Who's
FAMOUS
at YOUR
STATION?

Simon Ellinas
www.simonillustrations.com
www.londoncaricatures.com

Printed and bound in England

Who's FAMOUS *at YOUR* STATION?

Simon Ellinas

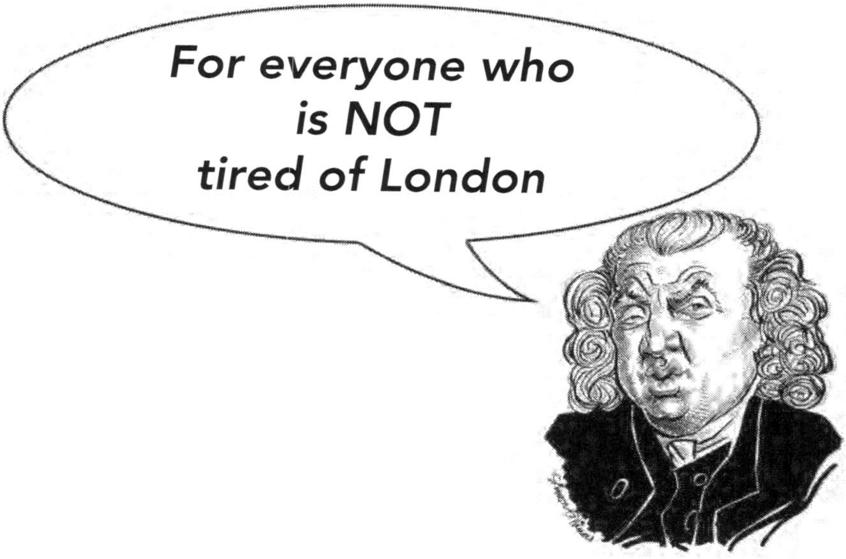
For everyone who is NOT tired of London

"In London, everyone is different, and that means anyone can fit in." – Paddington Bear

Contents

"There's nowhere else like London. Nothing at all, anywhere." – Vivienne Westwood

Introduction

WHO'S FAMOUS AT YOUR STATION began as a Lockdown project during the height of the pandemic in 2020. Instead of choosing to draw people randomly, I decided to research the area around each station to find interesting and famous people to caricature. London has been a magnet for great personalities of all types for centuries, so there were plenty to choose from. And, as I am a born and bred Londoner myself, the project was very close to my heart.

I have allocated a celebrity to every single station on the main London Underground network, creating 272 caricatures with a few short lines of biography and explanatory text.

Some of the facts may have changed by the time the book is in your hands (eg: the number of goals scored by Harry Kane!) but I have tried to ensure they are accurate. I welcome any suggestions for amendments for a second edition!

I hope you enjoy this book and keep it as a unique souvenir of one of the most vibrant, historical cities in the world.

A LITTLE BIT about me:

I'M A CARTOONIST and illustrator regularly published in national newspapers, magazines, books and websites. I also accept private commissions. I have lived and worked in London (and used the London Underground) all my life.

www.simonillustrations.com /
www.londoncaricatures.com

"London created the Underground, and the Underground created London" - John Lanchester, novelist and journalist

Bakerloo Line

Harrow and Wealdstone: Vinnie Jones

Birth Name: Vincent Peter Jones
Born: 5 January 1965
Best known as: Ex-professional footballer, actor and producer
Also: As a member of the "Crazy Gang" in Wimbledon Football club he helped the side win the 1988 FA Cup. His "hard man" acting career is characterized by his roles in Lock, Stock and Two Smoking Barrels and Snatch.
Link with area: Vinnie Jones was signed as a semi-professional by Wealdstone football club

Bakerloo Line

Kenton: Shami Chakrabarti

Birth Name: Sharmishta "Shami" Chakrabarti, Baroness Chakrabarti
Born: 16 June 1969
Best known as: Labour Party politician, barrister and human rights activist
Also: Considered by some as controversial, she sent her son to a fee-paying school after opposing the opening of new grammar schools because they "enforce segregation".
Link with area: Shami Chakrabarti was born in the area

Bakerloo Line

South Kenton: Denis Compton

Birth Name: Denis Charles Scott Compton
Born: 23 May 1918. Died: 23 April 1997
Best known as: Middlesex and England cricketer
Also: Professional footballer with Arsenal football club
Link with area: Denis Compton lived in the area

13

Bakerloo Line

North Wembley: Raheem Sterling

Birth Name: Raheem Shaquille Sterling
Born: 8 December 1994
Best known as: Professional footballer for Manchester City and England
Also: Awarded the Member of the Order of the British Empire for services to racial equality in sport
Link with area: Raheem Sterling grew up in North Wembley

Bakerloo Line

Wembley Central: Lenny Henry

Birth Name: Sir Lenworth George Henry
Born: 29 August 1958
Best known as: Comedian and actor known for co-founding Comic Relief
Also: He was married to Dawn French. He once said: "Ecstasy is a drug so powerful, it makes white people think they can dance."
Link with area: He lived in Wembley as a teenager

Bakerloo Line

Stonebridge Park: K.Koke

Birth Name: Kevin Georgiou, known professional as K.Koke
Born: 22 May 1985
Best known as: A rapper with Are you Alone
Also: His music career was halted when he was arrested for attempted murder although he was eventually acquitted of all charges
Link with area: K.Koke lives in Stonebridge Park

Bakerloo Line

Harlesden: Louis Theroux

Birth Name: Louis Sebastian Theroux
Born: 20 May 1970
Best known as: Documentary filmmaker, journalist and author, winner of two British Academy Television Awards and a Royal Television Society Television Award
Also: When Louis Met Jimmy Savile was voted one of the top documentaries of all time in 2005.
Link with area: Louis Theroux lived in Harlesden with his second wife and three sons

Willesden Junction: John Neville

Birth Name: John Reginald Neville
Born: 2 May 1925. Died: 19 November 2011
Best known as: Actor of stage and screen
Also: He became a Canadian citizen in the 1970s and became the artistic directors of various theatres
Link with area: Neville was born in Willesden

Bakerloo Line

Kensal Green: Phoebe Waller-Bridge

Birth Name: Phoebe Waller-Bridge
Born: 14 July 1985
Best known as: Creator, writer and star of BBC sitcom Fleabag and of Killing Eve
Also: Fleabag has won a whole host awards, including Emmys, British Academy
Television Awards, Golden Globes, Screen Actor Guild Awards, Critics Choice
Awards and Television Critics Association Awards
Link with area: She lived in Kensal Green for a few years before moving to New York

Bakerloo Line

Queen's Park: Cillian Murphy

Birth Name: Cillian Murphy
Born: 25 May 1976
Best known as: Actor playing Tommy Shelby in the BBC crime series Peaky Blinders
Also: He was a vegetarian for fifteen years because he "was worried about getting mad cow disease".
Link with area: He has lived there

Bakerloo Line

Kilburn Park: Gerry Anderson

Birth Name: Gerald Alexander Anderson
Born: 14 April 1929. Died: 26 December 2012
Best known as: Television and film producer of Thunderbirds, Stingray and Captain Scarlet
Also: Live action television series such as UFO and Space: 1999
Link with area: He spent his childhood there

Bakerloo Line

Maida Vale: Alan Turing

Birth Name: Alan Mathison Turing
Born: 23 June 1912. Died: 7 June 1954
Best known as: Mathematician who played a crucial part in cracking the German Enigma Code enabling the allies to defeat the Axis powers in many engagements. Also: he was prosecuted for homosexual acts. His death in 1954 from cyanide poisoning is thought to have been accidental although suicide was also suspected. Following an internet campaign and intervention from then Prime Minister Gordon Brown, The Queen granted Turing a posthumous pardon
Link with area: He was born there

Bakerloo Line

Warwick Avenue: Duffy

Birth Name: Aimee Anne Duffy
Born: 23 June 1984
Best known as: Singer/songwriter
Also: She won the Grammy Award for Best Pop Vocal Album for her album Rockferry
Link with area: She wrote a song about Warwick Avenue

Bakerloo Line

Paddington: Lucian Freud

Birth Name: Lucian Michael Freud
Born: 8 December 1922. Died: 20 July 2011
Best known as: painter and draughtsman.
Also: He's the grandson of Sigmund Freud. He's rumoured to have fathered as many as forty children through his many dalliances although only fourteen (!) have been officially verified
Link with area: He worked in a studio in Paddington

Bakerloo Line

Edgware Road: Montagu Pyke

Birth Name: Montagu Pyke
Born: 1874. Died: September 1935
Best known as: Cinema Entrepreneur who converted two shops at 164-166 Edgware Road into a cinema
Also: After expanding his cinema chain he became bankrupt in 1915 and an employee died in a fire at one of his venues. He was accused of manslaughter but was acquitted.
Link with area: He built a cinema there

Bakerloo Line

Marylebone: Ringo Starr

Birth Name: Richard Starkey
Born: 7 July 1940
Best known as: The drummer in the Beatles, writing and performing occasional songs such as Don't Pass Me By and Octopus's Garden
Also: A successful solo career (Back off Boogaloo) was followed by becoming the narrator for the Thomas the Tank Engine TV series
Link with area: Ringo Starr lived in Montagu Square for a while in the mid-1960s

Bakerloo Line

Regents Park: Damien Hirst

Birth Name: Damien Steven Hirst
Born: 7 June 1965
Best known as: Artist and entrepreneur famous for his dead shark, sheep and cow installations
Also: He had to apologise after congratulating the September 11 Twin Tower hijackers on a "visually stunning" work of art.
Link with area: Damien Hirst has a house there

Bakerloo Line

Lambeth North: Justin Welby

Birth Name: Justin Portal Welby
Born: 6 January 1956
Best known as: Archbishop of Canterbury
Also: He's interested in French culture, sailing and politics
Link with area: Lambeth Palace is the official London residence of the Archbishop of Canterbury

Central Line

West Ruislip: Andy Serkis

Birth Name: Andrew Clement Serkis
Born: 20 April 1964
Best known as: Gollum in Lord of the Rings
Also: Appeared as King Kong (2005) and as the ape Caesar in the Planet of the Apes films (2011- 2017)
Link with the area: He was born there

Central Line

Ruislip Gardens: Sue Holderness

Birth Name: Susan Joan Pringle Holderness
Born: 28 May 1949
Best known as: Marlene Boyce from television sitcom Only Fools and Horses
Link with the area: Moved to the area with parents during the Fifties

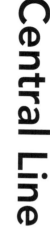

Central Line

South Ruislip: Adam Faith

Birth Name: Terence Nelhams Wright
Born: 23 June 1940. Died: 8 March 2003
Best known as: Singer (What Do You Want), actor (Budgie on TV) and financial journalist
Also: Film director Michael Winner claims that Faith was his financial adviser and that this led to significant losses
Link with the area: Adam Faith once lived there

Central Line

Northolt: Steve Perryman

Birth Name: Stephen John Perryman
Born: 21 December 1951
Best known as: Professional footballer with Tottenham Hotspur
Also: He is Tottenham's longest serving player, appearing 655 times
Link with the area: He grew up there

Greenford: Freddie Frinton

Birth Name: Frederick Bittiner Coo
Born: 17 January 1909. Died: 16 October 1968
Best known as: Comedian and actor in television sitcom Meet the Wife with Thora Hird. Also: His television short sketch Dinner For One, recorded in 1963 in Germany, has become hugely popular in Norway, Denmark, Finland, Estonia and Sweden on New Year's Eve for many years but was shown for the first time to a British audience in 2018 (Sky Arts)
Link with the area: He lived there

Central Line

Perivale: Rick Wakeman

Birth Name: Richard Christopher Wakeman
Born: 18 May 1949
Best known as: Keyboardist in progressive rock band Yes
Also: Known for his solo albums The Six Wives of Henry VIII and Journey To The Centre of the Earth amongst others
Link with the area: Born in Perivale opposite the iconic Hoover building

Central Line

Ealing Broadway: Shappi Khorsandi

Birth Name: Shaparak Khorsandi
Born: 8 June 1973
Best known as: Iranian-born British comedian and author
Also: A patron of Humanists UK
Link with the area: She lives in the area

Central Line

Hanger Lane: Keith Moon

Birth Name: Keith John Moon
Born: 23 August 1946. Died: 7 September 1978
Best known as: Drummer for the Who rock band
Also: known for his unique style, eccentric behaviour and drug addiction
Link with the area: He was born nearby

Central Line

West Acton: Alan Rickman

Birth Name: Alan Sidney Patrick Rickman
Born: 21 February 1946. Died: 14 January 2016
Best known as: Actor, well-known for the role of Professor Snape in the
Harry Potter films
Also: Empire magazine chose him as one of the 100 Sexiest Stars in film history (1995)
Link with the area: He was born in Acton

Central Line

North Acton: Arthur Lowe

Birth Name: Arthur Lowe
Born: 22 September 1915. Died: 15 April 1982
Best known as: Actor who played Captain Mainwaring in television comedy
Dad's Army
Also: He suffered from narcolepsy which caused him to fall asleep
during rehearsals
Link with the area: Dad's Army used to be rehearsed in a BBC studio in North Acton

Central Line

East Acton: Peter Ackroyd

Birth Name: Peter Ackroyd
Born: 5 November 1949
Best known as: Biographer, novelist and critic with works sucha as Hawksmoor and London, The Biography
Also: Particularly fascinated by London, he makes studies of its people and culture through history.
Link with the area: Born and raised on a council estate in East Acton by his mother and grandmother in a "strict Roman Catholic household"

Central Line

White City: Daisy Waugh

Birth Name: Daisy Louisa Dominica Waugh
Born: 19 February 1967
Best known as: Novelist and journalist. A recent novel is Phone For the Fish Knives
Also: The second daughter of writer and journalist Auberon Waugh. At time of writing thinking of setting up a yoga retreat in Costa Rica
Link with the area: Lives in White City

Central Line

Shepherd's Bush: Steve Jones

Birth Name: Stephen Philip Jones
Born: 3 September 1955
Best known as: Guitarist with the Sex Pistols
Also: has released solo albums and worked with Iggy Pop and Bob Dylan. Ranked 97th in "The 100 Greatest Guitarists of All Time" in Rolling Stone Magazine
Link with the area: Born in Shepherd's Bush where he lived with his hairdresser mother.

Central Line

Holland Park: Brian May

Birth Name: Brian Harold May
Born: 19 July 1947
Best known as: Guitarist with rock band Queen
Also: He studied Mathematics and Physics at Imperial College London and was awarded a PhD degree in astrophysics for work started in 1971 but only completed in 2007
Link with the area: He has a townhouse there in spite of his protests against neighbouring properties having basement developments.

Central Line

Notting Hill Gate: Stella McCartney

Birth Name: Stella Nina McCartney
Born: 13 September 1971
Best known as: Fashion designer daughter of singer-songwriter Paul McCartney
Also: Started Free Meat Monday, a non-profit campaign to raise awareness of the environmental impact of eating meat by encouraging people to have at least one meat-free day a week
Link with the area: She had a £2.5million townhouse there from 1998 to 2012 which she had to sell for £440k less than the asking price

Central Line

Queensway: Irfan Orga

Birth Name: Irfan Orga
Born: 31 October 1908. Died: 29 November 1970
Best known as: Turkish fighter pilot and author
Also: Portrait of a Turkish Family, published in 1950, was well received by John Betjeman and other literati.
Link with the area: He lived at 29, 35 and 221 Inverness Terrace from 1942 until the mid-fifties

Central Line

Lancaster Gate: Richard Seifert

Birth Name: Reubin Seifert
Born: 25 November 1910. Died: 26 October 2001
Best known as: Architect who designed Centre Point in London
Also: The designer of Tower 42 (the NatWest Tower) which was the tallest building in the City of London as well as many major office buildings in London and other major British cities
Link with the area: The Royal Lancaster Hotel tower was one of his creations

Central Line

Marble Arch: Claudia Winkleman

Birth Name: Claudia Anne Irena Winkleman
Born: 15 January 1972
Best known as: Television presenter, film critic and journalist. Best known for being co-presenter (with Tess Daly) of Strictly Come Dancing on BBC Television
Also: When her daughter's Hallowe'en costume caught fire, this prompted the government to tighten the flame retardant standards of Hallowe'en costumes
Link with the area: She has a house in the celebrity-rich Connaught Square. (Tony and Cherie Blair are also property owners here).

Central Line

Bond Street: Charles deGaulle

Birth Name: Charles André Joseph Marie de Gaulle
Born: 22 November 1890. Died: 9 November 1970
Best known as: President of France who was a wartime General in the French army
Also: He was particularly close to his younger brother Pierre, who so resembled him that his bodyguards often saluted him by mistake
Link with the area: De Gaulle was often in and around London and lived for a while in Hampstead, but his first London office was above the Cartier jewellery shop in Bond Street

Central Line

Oxford Circus: Bruce Forsyth

Birth Name: Bruce Joseph Forsyth-Johnson
Born: 22 February 1928. Died: 18 August 2017
Best known as: Veteran entertainer and presenter, most recently famous for presenting Strictly Come Dancing
Also: After coming to public attention through the ITV series Sunday Night at the London Palladium, he became a serial game show host including The Generation Game, Play Your Cards Right and The Price is Right.
Link with the area: Presenting Sunday Night at the London Palladium which is in Oxford Circus. His ashes have been buried under the stage there

Holborn: Naomi Lewis

Birth Name: Naomi Lewis
Born: 3 September 1911. Died: 5 July 2009
Best known as: Poet and literary critic
Also: Known for her translations of Hans Christian Andersen stories for children. She won the Eleanor Farjeon Award for distinguished service to the world of British children's books
Link with the area: A vegan and committed animal advocate, Naomi Lewis used to take injured pigeons to the restrooms of Conway Hall, in Holborn, to get them used to flying again

Central Line

Chancery Lane: Samuel Johnson

Birth Name: Samuel Johnson
Born: 18 September 1709. Died: 13 December 1784
Best known as: English writer who established the first English dictionary
Also: Well-known for his quotes such as ". . . when a man is tired of London, he is tired of life; for there is in London all that life can afford." He was a prolific writer of essays, poetry and biographies as well as being a seasoned literary critic
Link with the area: He lived in a house in Gough Square, now known as Dr Johnson's House

Central Line

St Paul's: Sir Christopher Wren

Birth Name: Christopher Wren
Born: 30 October 1632. Died: 8 March 1723
Best known as: Architect who designed St Paul's Cathedral in London
Also: He was an anatomist and astronomer. St Paul's was one of 52 churches he was charged with rebuilding after the Great Fire of London. He was at Westminster School with fellow architect and scientist Robert Hooke who collaborated with him on the building of the Monument in commemoration of the Great Fire of London
Link with the area: St Paul's Cathedral

Central Line

Liverpool Street: Tracey Emin

Birth Name: Tracey Karima Emin
Born: 3 July 1963
Best known as: Artist known for her autobiographical and confessional work
Also: A founder member of The Young British Artists in the 1980s, she is now a Royal Academician
Link with the area: She used to live in Tenter Ground, a four storey property in Spitalfields, near Liverpool Street. It was reportedly up for sale for £12million

Central Line

Bethnal Green: Helen Shapiro

Birth Name: Helen Kate Shapiro
Born: 28 September 1946
Best known as: Pop and Jazz singer, successful as a teenager in the 1960s
Also: Her hits included Don't Treat Me Like A Child and Tell Me What He Said and she toured with the Beatles in 1963
Link with the area: She was born at Bethnal Green Hospital

Central Line

Mile End: Piers Corbyn

Birth Name: Piers Richard Corbyn
Born: 10 March 1947
Best known as: Weather forecaster, anti-vaxxer and conspiracy theorist
Also: He's the brother of former Labour Party leader Jeremy Corbyn. He's a climate change and Covid-19 denier
Link with the area: He graduated with a degree in physics from Queen Mary University in Mile End

Central Line

Stratford: Christine Ohuruogu

Birth Name: Christine Ijeoma Ohuruogu
Born: 17 May 1984
Best known as: Olympic champion Track and field athlete
Also: She is also a former Commonwealth and World champion, specialising in the 400 metres race
Link with the area: She was raised less than a mile from the 2012 Summer Olympics in Stratford

Central Line

Leyton: Bobby Crush

Birth Name: Robert Nicholas "Bobby" Crush
Born: 23 March 1954
Best known as: Pianist, songwriter and television presenter
Also: He came to attention through Hughie Green's TV show Opportunity Knocks in 1972
Link with the area: He was born in Leyton and attended Leyton county High School for Boys

Central Line

Leytonstone: Alfred Hitchcock

Birth Name: Alfred Joseph Hitchcock
Born:13 August 1899. Died: 29 April 1980
Best known as: Film director and influential figure in cinema
Also: He directed over fifty feature films and earned the title of 'Master of Suspense', with such classics as Psycho, The Birds, Rear Window and North by Northwest just a few of the masterpieces in his oeuvre.
Link with the area: He was born in a flat above his parents' grocer's shop at 517 High Road Leytonstone

Central Line

Snaresbrook: Rev Andrew Reed

Birth Name: Andrew Reed
Born: 27 November 1787. Died: 25 February 1862
Best known as: An English Congregational minister and hymnwriter
Also: A philanthropist and social reformer who voiced opposition to slavery in America
Link with the area: He commissioned the building of the Infant Orphan Asylum in Hollybush Hill, Snaresbrook

South Woodford: Sanjeev Bhaskar

Birth Name: Sanjeev Bhaskar
Born: 31 October 1963
Best known as: Actor, comedian and television presenter
Also: best known for the television shows Goodness Gracious Me and The Kumars at No. 42
Link with the area: He lives in South Woodford with his family

Central Line

Woodford: James Hilton

Birth Name: James Hilton
Born: 9 September 1900. Died: 20 December 1954
Best known as: Novelist best known for Goodbye Mr Chips
Also: He also wrote screenplays for Hollywood, winning an Academy Award for his work on the script of Mrs Miniver which starred Greer Garson and Walter Pidgeon
Link with the area: He lived at 42 Oak Hill Gardens Woodford

Central Line

Buckhurst Hill: Jack Straw

Birth Name: Jack Whitaker Straw
Born: 3 August 1946
Best known as: Political and Cabinet member in Labour Governments of Tony Blair and Gordon Brown
Also: He was Home Secretary from 1997 to 2001 and Foreign Secretary from 2001 to 2006
Link with the area: He was born there

Central Line

Loughton: Alan Davies

Birth Name: Alan Roger Davies
Born: 6 March 1966
Best known as: Comedian, actor and television presenter
Also: Best known as a panellist on the quiz show QI chaired by Stephen Fry and
Sandi Toksvig and for playing the title role in the mystery series Jonathan Creek
Link with the area: He was born in Loughton and attended Staples Road Primary
School there

Central Line

Debden: Danny Dyer

Birth Name: Daniel John Dyer
Born: 24 July 1977
Best known as: Actor and presenter best known for being part of the BBC soap opera Eastenders
Also: In the BBC's Who do You Think You Are he found out that he is the direct descendant of both Thomas Cromwell and every English king from William Conqueror to Edward III
Link with the area: He lives there

Central Line

Theydon Bois: Harry Kane

Birth Name: Harry Edward Kane
Born: 28 July 1993
Best known as: Professional footballer for Tottenham Hotspur and as captain of the England national team
Also: At the time of writing, he has scored 49 goals in 68 appearances for England, being well on the way to breaking the England men's goal record
Link with the area: He lives there in a £17million mansion

Central Line

Epping: Rod Stewart

Birth Name: Sir Roderick David Stewart
Born: 10 January 1945
Best known as: a raspy voiced rock and pop singer
Also: he is a songwriter and one of the best-selling music artists of all time, having
sold over 250 million records worldwide, including Do Ya Think I'm Sexy
and Sailing.
Link with the area: Rod lived at Copped Hall, Epping for over 30 years.

Central Line

Wanstead: Jimi Hendrix

Birth Name: James Marshall "Jimi" Hendrix
Born: 27 November 1942. Died: September 18 1970
Best known as: guitarist, singer and songwriter
Also: Widely regarded as one of the most gifted and influential electric guitarists in
the history of popular music, producing songs such as Hey Joe and The Wind
Cries Mary
Link with the area: After seeing the marsh gases rising from Wanstead flats, he
wrote Purple Haze in the nearby Upper Cut Club where he was performing

Central Line

Redbridge: Keith Flint

Birth Name: Keith Charles Flint
Born: 17 September 1969. Died: 4 March 2019
Best known as: Singer, dancer and motorcycle racer
Also: Frontman of electronic dance band The Prodigy and performed on their two number one singles Firestarter and Breathe
Link with the area: He was born in Redbridge

Central Line

Gants Hill: Richard Littlejohn

Birth Name: Richard Littlejohn
Born: 18 January 1954
Best known as: Journalist for the Daily Mail, author and broadcaster
Also: Often accused of insufficient fact-checking he would often us the phrase "you couldn't make it up" for many items in his columns
Link with the area: Richard Littlejohn lives in Gants Hill

Central Line

Newbury Park: Victor Maddern

Birth Name: Victor Jack Maddern
Born: 16 march 1928. Died: 22 June 1993
Best known as: Actor, often in military roles
Also: He ran a script printing business and opened a public speaking school
offering special rates to Conservative MPs and constituency workers
Link with the area: He lived there

Central Line

Barkingside: Kathy Kirby

Birth Name: Catherine Ethel O'Rourke
Born: 20 October 1938. Died: 19 May 2011
Best known as: Singer best known for Secret Love which was originally recorded by
Doris Day
Also: Represented the United Kingdom in the 1965 Eurovision Song Contest,
finishing in second place
Link with the area: Kathy Kirby grew up in Barkingside

Fairlop: Queen Anne, of Great Britain

Birth Name: Anne
Born: 6 February 1665. Died: 1 August 1714
Best known as: Queen of England, Scotland and Ireland between 8 March 1702 and
1 May 1707. She succeeded to the throne after the death of her cousin William III
Also: She failed to produce an heir in spite of of seventeen pregnancies
Link with the area: Legend has it that Queen Anne visited The Fairlop Oak which was
a notable tree which grew near Fairlop station

Central Line

Simon Ollinas

Grange Hill: Alan Sugar

Birth Name: Alan Michael Sugar
Born: 24 March 1947
Best known as: Businessman founder of company, Amstrad and host of the television show The Apprentice
Also: His fortune is estimated at £1.2billion making him the 121st-richest person in the UK
Link with the area: He lives in Grange Hill

Central Line

Hainault: Jimmy Greaves

Birth Name: James Peter Greaves
Born: 20 February 1940. Died: 19 September 20121
Best known as: Professional footballer for Tottenham Hotspur and the England
national team
Also: He presented a popular television football show with Ian St John called Saint
and Greavesie
Link with the area: He was raised in Hainault

Central Line

Chigwell: Sally Gunnell

Birth Name: Sally Jane Janet Gunnell
Born: 29 July 1966
Best known as: Olympic Gold winning track and field athlete (400 metres hurdles)
Also: The only female British athlete to have won Olympic, World, European and Commonwealth titles
Link with the area: Sally Gunnell was born in Chigwell

Roding Valley: Mark Wright

Birth Name: Mark Charles Edward Wright
Born: 20 January 1987
Best known as: Television personality who came to public attentions through The Only Way is Essex (TOWIE)
Also: He was a semi-professional footballer, starting his senior career with Southend United
Link with the area: He went to Roding Valley High School

Circle Line

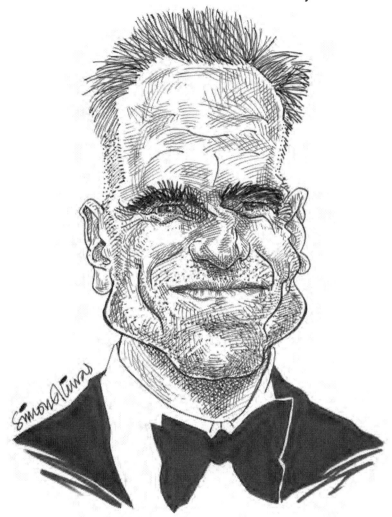

High Street Kensington: Daniel Day-Lewis

Birth Name: Daniel Michael Blake Day-Lewis
Born: 29 April 1957
Best known as: Award winning English actor
Also: He won the best actor Academy Award for My Left Foot, There Will Be Blood
and Lincoln. He's the first and only acts to have on that category three times. He's
won multiple other awards including British Academy Film Awards, Golden Globes,
Screen Actors Guild Awards and Critics' Choice Awards amongst others
Link with the area: The family home was nearby

Circle Line

Bayswater: Adrian Edmondson and Rik Mayall

Birth Names: Adrian Edmondson and Rik Mayall
Born: 24 Jan 1957 (Edmondson); 7 March 1958 (Mayall). Rik Mayall Died: 9 June 2014
Best known as: Comedians and actors who starred in the television seres The
Young Ones.
Also: Other credits include The Comic Strip Presents . . . and Bottom. Individually,
Mayall became well-known for The New Statesman and Edmondson had a lead role
in Doctors and Nurses. Edmondson pursued a musical career with his punk folk band
The Bad Shepherds and a comedy ensemble band with Neil Innes and Rowland
Rivron, The Idiot Bastard Band
Link with the area: Both had houses in the area

Circle Line

Sloane Square: Jemima Goldsmith

Birth Name: Jemima Marcelle Goldsmith
Born: 30 January 1974
Best known as: Screenwriter and television producer
Also: The daughter of financier Sir James Goldsmith, she was formerly a journalist on such publications as New Statesman and Vanity Fair. She was married to the current Prime Minister of Pakistan, Imran Khan.
Link with the area: She used to be one of the original 'Sloane Rangers' spending a lot of time in the area

St James' Park: King Charles II

Birth Name: Charles
Born: 29 May 1630. Died: 6 February 1685
Best known as: King of Scotland from 1649 to 1651 and King of Scotland, England and Ireland from 1660 to 1685
Also: He had to flee to Europe during the rule of Oliver Cromwell and it was only after Cromwell's death in 1658, that the Restoration of the Monarchy occurred and he was installed as King in 1660
Link with the area: He was responsible for re-designing St James' Park with avenues of trees planted and lawns laid

79

Circle Line

Temple: John Mortimer

Birth Name: John Clifford Mortimer
Born: 21 April. Died: 16 January 2009
Best known as: A barrister, dramatist and writer of novels about a barrister named Horace Rumpole
Also: He defended the editors of the satirical paper Oz against charges of a "conspiracy to corrupt"
Link with the area: He used to practice as a barrister in the area

Circle Line

Blackfriars: Richard Burbage

Birth Name: Richard Burbage
Born: c. 1567. Died: 13 March 1619
Best known as: Stage actor well-known for appearing at the Globe Theatre
Also: A theory has it that Shakespeare based Hamlet on Richard Burbage and not
on his own son Hamnet and Burbage was the first actor to play the role
Link with the area: Blackfriars Theatre was built by his father James Burbage and
Richard Burbage was one of seven sharers in it including William Shakespeare

Circle Line

Mansion House: William Russell

Birth Name: William Anthony Bowater Russell
Born: 15 April 1965
Best known as: Financier who served as Lord Mayor of the City of London from 2019 to 2021
Also: Served a second term as Lord Mayor because of the Covid-19 crisis; the first person to serve two terms since William Cubitt in 1861
Link with the area: Mansion House is the official residence and office of the Lord Mayor of London

Circle Line

Cannon Street: Alexandre de Rothschild

Birth Name: Alexandre Guy Francesco de Rothschild
Born: 3 December 1980
Best known as: Executive Chairman of Rothschild and Co merchant bankers
Also: A descendant of the Rothschild family who rose to prominence with Mayer
Amschel Rothschild (1744-1812) from Frankfurt
Link with the area: His office is in the area

Circle Line

Monument: Robert Hooke

Birth Name: Robert Hooke
Born: 18 July 1635. Died: 3 March 1703
Best known as: Scientist and architect who was the first to visualise a micro-organism using a microscope
Also: He worked with Samuel Pepys on rebuilding London after The Great Fire in 1666, notably on the construction of the Monument
Link with the area: He helped to build The Monument

Circle Line

Tower Hill: David Suchet

Birth Name: David Courtney Suchet
Born: 2 May 1946
Best known as: Actor who portrayed Agatha Christie's Hercule Poirot in the television adaptations
Also: He was nominated for a BAFTA for his portrayal of Poirot and won an International Emmy Award for Best Actor for his role as Robert Maxwell in the 2007 television film Maxwell
Link with the area: He used to have a flat in nearby St Katharine Docks

Circle Line

Aldgate: Daniel Mendoza

Birth Name: Daniel Mendoza
Born: 5 July 1764. Died: 3 September 1836
Best known as: Prizefighter who became the 18th boxing champion of England
from 1792 - 1795
Also: He also worked as a glass cutter, labourer and greengrocer in the East End
Link with the area: He was born there

Barbican: Norman Tebbit

Birth Name: Norman Beresford Tebbit
Born: 29 March 1931
Best known as: Politician and Cabinet minister in the Conservative government of
Margaret Thatcher and for being misquoted as having told the unemployed to
"get on your bike"
Also: He was injured in the IRA bombing of the Grand Hotel Brighton during the
1984 Conservative Party conference
Link with the area: He lived in the Barbican Estate

Circle Line

Farringdon: Keith Reilly

Birth Name: Keith Reilly
Born: 1959
Best known as: Co-founder of London club Fabric
Also: A DJ owning more than 500,000 vinyl records
Link with the area: The club, Fabric, is located in Charterhouse Street close to
Farringdon station

Euston Square: Alexei Sayle

Birth Name: Alexei David Sayle
Born: 7 August 1952
Best known as: Comedian, actor and author with TV series such as Stuff and The All New Alexei Sayle Show
Also: A leading figure in the alternative comedy movement in the 1980s
Link with the area: He has a house there

Circle Line

Great Portland Street: Carl Von Weber

Birth Name: Carl Maria Friedrich Ernst von Weber
Born: 18/19 November 1786. Died: 5 June 1826
Best known as: Composer and musician
Also: Best known for his operas
Link with the area: He died in a house nearby

Circle Line

Edgware Road: Joe Strummer

Birth Name: John Graham Mellor
Born: 21 August 1952. Died: 22 December 2002
Best known as: Musician with The Clash
Also: Stints with The 101ers, Latino Rockabilly War, The Mescaleros and The
Pogues and solo performances whcih included soundtracks for films
Link with the area: Joe Strummer used to busk in the subway between the two
Edgware Road stations

Circle Line

Royal Oak: Thomas Hardy

Birth Name: Thomas Hardy
Born: 2 June 1840. Died: 11 January 1928
Best known as: Novelist and poet
Also: famous for novels such as Far from the Madding Crowd, Tess of the
d'Urbervilles and The Mayor of Casterbridge, often set in the semi-fictional region
of Wessex
Link with the area: He lived briefly at 4 Celbridge Place (later Porchester Road)

Westbourne Park: Michael Gove

Birth Name: Michael Andrew Gove
Born: 26 August 1967
Best known as: Politician and member of the Conservative cabinet
Also: Secretary of State for Levelling Up, he has run for leadership of the
Conservative party twice, finishing in third place on both occasions
Link with the area: Used to live in the area straddling Westbourne Park and
Notting Hill

Circle Line

Ladbroke Grove: Chrissie Hynde

Birth Name: Christine Ellen Hyde
Born: 7 September 1951
Best known as: Singer-songwriter and musician
Also: Founder member, guitarist and vocalist for the Pretenders rock band who had a big hit with Brass in Pocket
Link with the area: She has lived there

Circle Line

Latimer Road: Joss Ackland

Birth Name: Sidney Edmond Jocelyn "Joss" Ackland
Born: 29 February 1928
Best known as: An actor
Also: Known for his appearance on television in The Adventures of Sherlock
Holmes with Jeremy Brett and for many film, stage and television appearances
Link with the area: He was born there

Circle Line

Wood Lane: John Birt

Birth Name: John Birt
Born: 10 December 1944
Best known as: Television executive and businessman
Also: As Director-General, he restructured the BBC and paved the way for digital broadcasting
Link with the area: The BBC offices are in Wood Lane

Shepherd's Bush Market: Evelyn Glennie

Birth Name: Evelyn Elizabeth Ann Glennie
Born: 19 July 1965
Best known as: Percussionist
Also: Well-known for being profoundly deaf and playing barefoot to feel the music.
Won the Best Classical Instrument Solo award in the 2014 Grammys
Link with the area: She lives there

Circle Line

Goldhawk Road: Daniel Radcliffe

Birth Name: Daniel Jacob Radcliffe
Born: 23 July 1989
Best known as: Actor in the Harry Potter films (as Harry Potter)
Also: Multi-award winning and nominated, including Breakout Movie Actor for the Teen Choice Awards in 2001 and nomination for the Best Hero in the National Movie Awards in 2006.
Link with the area: Born in Queen Charlotte's Hospital, Goldhawk Road

District Line

Upminster: Richard Johnson

Birth Name: Richard Keith Johnson
Born: 30 July 1927. Died: 5 June 2015
Best known as: Actor, writer and producer
Also: An accomplished Shakespearian actor, Johnson also starred in many films, notably, The Haunting, Khartoum and Oedipus the King
Link with the area: He was born there

District Line

Upminster Bridge: Ian Dury

Birth Name: Ian Robins Dury
Born: 12 May 1942. Died: 27 March 2000
Best known as: Singer-songwriter of the 1970s punk era
Also: Best known songs were Hit Me With Your Rhythm Stick and Reasons to be Cheerful
Link with the area: He moved there when he was three-years-old

100

District Line

Hornchurch: Kenny Ball

Birth Name: Kenneth Daniel Ball
Born: 22 May 1930. Died: 7 March 2013
Best known as: Jazz musician scoring hits with The Green Leaves of Summer and Samantha
Also: Bandleader and lead trumpet player in Kenny Ball and his Jazzmen
Link with the area: He was born there

District Line

Elm Park: Sir Harry Broadhurst

Birth Name: Sir Harry Broadhurst
Born: 28 October 1905. Died: 29 August 1995
Best known as: Royal Air Force Commander and flying ace of the Second World War gaining a reputation as an aerial daredevil
Also: In 1959 he became Commander, Allied Air Forces Central Europe before retiring to become managing director of Hawker Siddeley Aviation Ltd.
Link with the area: Lived there whilst in command of RAF Hornchurch

District Line

Dagenham East: George Carey

Birth Name: George Leonard Carey
Born: 13 November 1935
Best known as: Archbishop of Canterbury from 1991 to 2002
Also: He presided over the ordination of the first women priests in the Church of England
Link with the area: He attended Bonham Road Primary School there

District Line

Dagenham Heathway: Dudley Moore

Birth Name: Dudley Stuart John Moore
Born: 19 April 1935. Died: 27 March 2002
Best known as: Comedian, actor and musician
Also: Came to prominence with the comedy revue Beyond The Fringe which
led to his partnership with Peter Cook in Not Only But Also on television for
which they won the British Academy Television Award for Best
Entertainment Performance
Link with the area: He was brought up there

District Line

Becontree: Sir Alf Ramsey

Birth Name: Alfred Ernest Ramsey
Born: 22 January 1920. Died: 28 April 1999
Best known as: England football manager from 1963 to 1974
Also: Guided the England team to victory in the World Cup in 1966
Link with the area: He's commemorated with a plaque on the Becontree Estate

District Line

Upney: Ross Kemp

Birth Name: Ross James Kemp
Born: 21 July 1964
Best known as: Actor, author and television presenter
Also: He played the part of Grant Mitchell in Eastenders for which he won the Best
Actor Award at several awards ceremonies including British Soap Awards. His
documentary Ross Kemp on Gangs won the Best Factual Series Award at
the BAFTAs
Link with the area: Born on the Upney side of Barking

District Line

Aldgate East: Ronnie Scott

Birth Name: Ronald Schatt
Born: 28 January 1927. Died: 23 December 1996
Best known as: Jazz saxophonist and jazz club owner
Also: He used to say of his club: "I love this place, it's just like home, filthy and full of strangers."
Link with the area: He was born there

District Line

West Brompton: Bernard Levin

Birth Name: Henry Bernard Levin
Born: 19 August 1928. Died: 7 August 2004
Best known as: Journalist, author and broadcaster
Also: His career as a broadcaster began with That Was The Week That Was
followed by Face the Music. In 1962, he was famously punched by ex-RAF pilot
Desmond Leslie, in protest against Levin's critical review one of his actress wife's
performances
Link with the area: He's buried in Brompton Cemetery

District Line

Kensington Olympia: David Lloyd George

Birth Name: David Lloyd George
Born: 17 January 1863. Died: 26 March 1945
Best known as: Liberal politician and UK Prime Minister from 1916 - 1922
Also: A skilled orator who was a champion for Welsh devolution and the
disestablishment of the Anglican church. He was Minister for Munitions during the
the First World War and was a major player in the Paris Peace Conference of 1919.
Consequently, feeling that Germany had been treated unfairly, he misguidedly
became sympathetic towards Hitler
Link with the area: He had a house nearby

District Line

Fulham Broadway: Jessica Martin

Birth Name: Jessica Cecelia Anna Maria Martin
Born: 25 August 1962
Best known as: Actress, singer, impressionist and comic writer and illustrator
Also: A prolific performer during the eighties on television variety shows such as Bobby Davro On The Box and multiple stage appearances in musicals in the West End. Her illustrated books bring the glamour of old Hollywood back to life with titles such as It Girl about silent movie star Clara Bow
Link with the area: She was born there

110

District Line

Parsons Green: Pippa Middleton

Birth Name: Philippa Charlotte Middleton
Born: 6 September 1983
Best known as: Socialite, author and columnist
Also: She is the younger sister of Catherine, the Duchess of Cambridge
Link with the area: She lived in the area for a while with former boyfriend
Nico Jackson

District Line

Putney Bridge: Fred Russell

Birth Name: Thomas Frederick Parnell
Born: 29 September 1862. Died: 14 October 1957
Best known as: Ventriloquist known as "The Father of Modern Ventriloquism"
Also: He started working life as a journalist, becoming editor of the Hackney and Kingsland Gazette
Link with the area: He lived there in a flat

District Line

East Putney: Leonard Woolf

Birth Name: Leonard Sidney Woolf
Born: 25 November 1880
Died: 14 August 1969
Best known as: Author, publisher and political theorist
Also: Known for his novel The Village in the Jungle and, with his wife, Virginia Woolf, establishing the Hogarth Press publishing company
Link with the area: He lived there with his family from 1894 - 1914

District Line

Southfields: Andy Hamilton

Birth Name: Andrew Neil Hamilton
Born: 28 May 1954
Best known as: Broadcaster, television director and comedy writer who wrote Old Harry's Game for BBC Radio 4 and co-wrote Drop the Dead Donkey for Channel Four
Also: He has no thumb on his right hand. He has said it was amputated "by a surgeon who felt that symmetry was over-rated."
Link with the area: Has been living there since 2005

District Line

Wimbledon Park: Serena Williams

Birth Name: Serena Jameka Williams
Born: September 26 1981
Best known as: American professional tennis player
Also: Winner of 23 Grand Slam singles titles and considered one of the greatest tennis players of all time
Link with the area: She's won the Wimbledon singles title seven times

115

Wimbledon: Raymond Briggs

Birth Name: Raymond Redvers Briggs
Born: 18 January 1934
Best known as: Illustrator, cartoonist and author
Also: Well-known writing and illustrating Fungus the Bogeyman, The Snowman and When the Wind Blows
Link with the area: He grew up in the area

District Line

West Kensington: William Butler Yeats

Birth Name: William Butler Yeats
Born: 13 June 1865. Died: 28 January 1939
Best known as: Poet, famous for He Wishes for the Cloths of Heaven
Also: Helped to establish the Abbey Theatre in Dublin and won the Nobel Prize in Literature in 1923 "for his always inspired poetry"
Link with the area: He and his family lived there from 1874 - 1876

District Line

Ravenscourt Park: Carrie Johnson

Birth Name: Carrie Louise Bevan Symonds
Born: 17 March 1988
Best known as: Wife of Prime Minster Boris Johnson
Also: Known as a political and climate activist and is a senior advisor to the ocean conservation charity Oceana
Link with the area: She attended Godolphin and Latymer School near to Ravenscourt Park

District Line

Stamford Brook: Trevor Nunn

Birth Name: Trevor Robert Nunn
Born: 14 January 1940
Best known as: Theatre director who has been Artistic Director for the Royal Shakespeare Company, The Royal National Theatre and, currently the Theatre Royal, Haymarket
Also: Multi-award winning including, amongst others, A Tony Award for Cats (1983), Les Miserables (1987) and Olivier Awards for productions of Troilus and Cressida (2000) and Nicholas Nickleby (1980)
Link with the area: He has a house near there

District Line

Chiswick Park: Kate Humble

Birth Name: Katherine Mary Humble
Born: 12 December 1968
Best known as: Television presenter specialising in wildlife programmes
Also: Known for presenting Countryfile and Kate Humble's Coastal Britain, she was appointed President of the Royal Society for the Protection of Birds from 2009 - 2013
Link with the area: She lived there before moving to a smallholding in Wales

District Line

Gunnersbury: Tony Slattery

Birth Name: Tony Declan James Slattery
Born: 9 November 1959
Best known as: Actor and comedian who was a regular on Whose Line Is It Anyway plus performances, both comedy and serious in The Crying Game, Peter's Friends and How to Get Ahead in Advertising
Also: He was part of the Cambridge Footlights at the same time as Stephen Fry, Emma Thompson and Hugh Laurie
Link with the area: He was educated at Gunnersbury Boys' Grammar School

District Line

Kew Gardens: Gabby Logan

Birth Name: Gabrielle Nicole Logan
Born: 24 April 1973
Best known as: Television Sports presenter for the BBC
Also: She's a former international rhythmic gymnast and won the Sports Presenter of the Year four times (2000, 2002, 2004 and 2014) at the Television and Radio Industries Club Awards
Link with the area: She used to live there

District Line

Richmond: Ronnie Wood

Birth Name: Ronald David Wood
Born: 1 June 1947
Best known as: Rock musician/guitarist for the Rolling Stones
Also: An enthusiastic painter who was once at Ealing Art College, his artworks, featuring icons of popular culture have been exhibited all over the world
Link with the area: He used to live in Wick House after being it from actor Sir John Mills and then sold it to The Who's Pete Townshend

Hammersmith and City Line

Barking: Billy Bragg

Birth Name: Stephen William Bragg
Born: 20 December 1957
Best known as: Singer-songwriter and left-wing activist who often did benefit gigs for the miners' strike in 1984. His 'signature song' is said to be New England
Also: Currently concentrating on the environment, the rise of the populist right and how the gig economy is "pushing people to the margins of society"
Link with the area: It was his childhood home

Hammersmith and City Line

East Ham: Gerald Scarfe

Birth Name: Gerald Anthony Scarfe
Born: 1 June 1936
Best known as: Cartoonist and illustrator
Also: Has worked as the editorial cartoonist for The Sunday Times and illustrator for The New Yorker. He carried out reportage assignments in Vietnam, the Middle East, India and Northern Ireland. He is married to actress Jane Asher
Link with the area: He attended East Ham Technical College (now Newham College of Further Education)

Hammersmith and City Line

Upton Park: Trevor Brooking

Birth Name: Trevor David Brooking
Born: 2 October 1948
Best known as: Footballer, manager and pundit
Also: He was mostly at West Ham United winning the FA Cup in 1975 and 1980
Link with the area: West Ham United Football Club was situated there

Hammersmith and City Line

Plaistow: Honor Blackman

Birth Name: Honor Blackman
Born: 22 August 1925. Died: 5 April 2020
Best known as: Actress in The Avengers (as Cathy Gale) and Goldfinger
(Pussy Galore)
Also: She was in the television sitcom The Upper Hand from 1990 to 1996
Link with the area: She was born there

Hammersmith and City Line

Bromley-by-Bow: Ashley Cole

Birth Name: Ashley Cole
Born: 20 December 1980
Best known as: Former footballer for Chelsea, Arsenal and England
Also: He is currently a coach at Everton football club
Link with the area: He went to Bow School in the area

Hammersmith and City Line

Bow Road: Dizzee Rascal

Birth Name: Dylan Kwabena Mills
Born: 18 September 1984
Best known as: Rapper, songwriter and record producer
Also: His album Boy in da Corner won the Mercury Prize Best Album of the Year in 2003 and his Bop N' Keep It Dippin won the Best Music Video at The Webby Awards in 2018
Link with the area: He was born and brought up in the area

Hammersmith and City Line

Stepney Green: Steven Berkoff

Birth Name: Leslie Steven Berks
Born: 2 August 1937
Best known as: Actor, playwright and director known for his 'expressionistic' style
Also: In films he has appeared in A Clockwork Orange, McVicar, Absolute Beginners and Legionnaire amongst others. His play Kvetch won the Evening Standard Theatre Award for Best Comedy in 1997 and was nominated for a Society of London Theatre's Laurence Olivier Award for Best Entertainment for his one-man show Shakespeare's Villains
Link with the area: He was born there

Hammersmith and City Line

Whitechapel: Micky Flanagan

Birth Name: Michael John Flanagan
Born: 7 October 1962
Best known as: Comedian
Also: He was nominated for Best Newcomer at the Edinburgh Comedy Awards in 2007. A regular panellist on shows such as Mock the Week, 8 Out Of 10 Cats and A League of Their Own
Link with the area: He was born there

Hammersmith and City Line

Paddington: Alexander Fleming

Birth Name: Alexander Fleming
Born: 6 August 1881. Died: 11 March 1955
Best known as: The discoverer of penicillin
Also: For this discovery he shared the Nobel Prize in Physiology or medicine in 1945 with Howard Florey and Ernst Boris Chain
Link with the area: The laboratory where penicillin was discovered is here and can now be visited as the Alexander Fleming Laboratory Museum

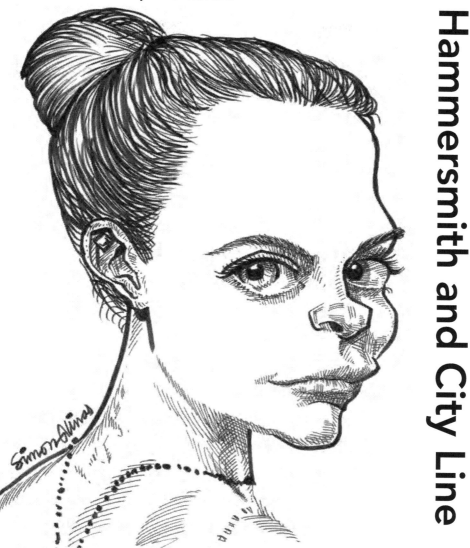

Hammersmith and City Line

Hammersmith: Cara Delevingne

Birth Name: Cara Jocelyn Delevingne
Born: 12 August 1992
Best known as: Model, actress and singer
Also: She won the Model of the Year at the British Fashion Awards in 2012 and
2014. She openly identifies as bisexual and pansexual
Link with the area: She was born there

Jubilee Line

Stanmore: Roger Moore

Birth Name: Roger George Moore
Born: 14 October 1927. Died: 23 may 2017
Best known as: Actor well-known for portraying the third James Bond in films
Also: On television he was Simon Templar in the series The Saint. He is credited with inspiring the Magnum ice cream after saying that his one wish would be for "a choc ice on a stick".
Link with the area: He lived there

Jubilee Line

Canons Park: Darren Currie

Birth Name: Darren Paul Currie
Born: 29 November 1974
Best known as: Former footballer connected to many clubs including West Ham United for whom he played no first team games, Shrewsbury Town, Barnet and Hendon
Also: He has managed Dagenham and Redbridge, Barnet and Sheffield United (U23)
Link with the area: Barnet Football Club's grounds are there

Jubilee Line

Queensbury: Amy Johnson

Birth Name: Amy Johnson
Born: 1 July 1903. Disappeared: 5 January 1941
Best known as: Pilot who was the first woman to fly solo from London to Australia
Also: Her disappearance in 1941 as her plane crashed into the Thames estuary near Herne Bay is hotly discussed. Some say she was shot down as she was mistaken for an enemy aircraft, others say she was sucked into the propellers of the ship attempting to rescue her
Link with the area: She learned to fly at the flying school in Stag Lane in Queensbury

Jubilee Line

Kingsbury: Charlie Watts

Birth Name: Charles Robert Watts
Born: 2 June 1941. Died: 24 August 2021
Best known as: The drummer with the Rolling Stones
Also: He had his own jazz bands, the Charlie Watts Quintet and the Charlie Watts Tentet. He is often regarded as one of the greatest drummers of all time
Link with the area: He attended Tylers Croft Boys Secondary Modern, now a part of Kingsbury High School.

Jubilee Line

Wembley Park: Riz Ahmed

Birth Name: Rizwan Ahmed
Born: 1 December 1982
Best known as: Actor and rapper who came to attention in Four Lions
Also: Achieved international recognition for his role in Nightcrawler alongside Jake Gyllenhaal. He's won the Best Male Lead for Sound of Metal (2021) at the Independent Spirit Awards and the Outstanding Lead Actor in a Limited Series or Movie from the Primetime Emmy Wards for The Night Of (2017)
Link with the area: He was born in Wembley

Jubilee Line

Neasden: Twiggy

Birth Name: Lesley lawson (née Hornby)
Born: 19 September 1949
Best known as: Model, actress and singer
Also: Her hairdresser boyfriend Justin de Villeneuve (originally Nigel Davies) is credited with discovering Twiggy and for persuading her to change her name. She won two Golden Globe Awards for her role in The Boyfriend (1971)
Link with the area: She was born there

Jubilee Line

Dollis Hill: David Baddiel

Birth Name: David Lionel Baddiel
Born: 28 May 1964
Best known as: Comedian, presenter and author
Also: Known for The Mary Whitehouse Experience, Newman and Baddiel and his comedy partnership with Frank Skinner, as lifelong football fans. He has written four novels including Whatever Love Means with its references to Princess Diana's death
Link with the area: He grew up in Dollis Hill

Jubilee Line

Willesden Green: Rod Price

Birth Name: Roderick Michael Price
Born: 22 November 1947. Died: 22 March 2005
Best known as: Guitarist with rock band Foghat
Also: He was an exponent of slide guitar and so was known as the 'Magician of Slide' and 'Slide King of Rock And Roll'
Link with the area: He was born there

Kilburn: A.A. Milne

Birth Name: Alan Alexander Milne
Born: 18 January 1882. Died: 31 January 1956
Best known as: Author of the Winnie-the-Pooh books
Also: A regular contributor to Punch, he produced the children's poems When We
Were Very Young in collaboration with Punch staff cartoonist E. H. Shepard, a
partnership that was to continue in the Winnie-the-Pooh books
Link with the area: He was born there

142

Jubilee Line

West Hampstead: Emma Thompson

Birth Name: Emma Thompson
Born: 15 April 1959
Best known as: Actress and screenwriter
Also: Daughter of the Magic Roundabout (English) creator and narrator, Eric Thompson, her role in Howards End won best Actress awards from the Academy Awards, The Golden Globes and BAFTA, amongst many other awards during her career
Link with the area: She lives there

Jubilee Line

Finchley Road: Sigmund Freud

Birth Name: Sigmund Schlomo Freud
Born: 6 May 1856. Died: 23 September 1939
Best known as: Neurologist founder of psychoanalysis
Also: He formulated the Oedipus complex and the analysis of dreams. The method of dialogue between patient and psychoanalyst was pioneered by Freud
Link with the area: He lived there and his house is now the Freud Museum

Jubilee Line

Swiss Cottage: Katya Adler

Birth Name: Michal Katya Adler
Born: 3 May 1972
Best known as: Journalist and BBC political correspondent (mostly for Europe)
Also: She was awarded the Charles Wheeler award for Outstanding Contribution to
Broadcast Journalism in 2019
Link with the area: She went to South Hampstead High School which is nearby

Jubilee Line

St John's Wood: Keith Richards

Birth Name: Keith Richards
Born: 18 December 1943
Best known as: Guitarist with the Rolling Stones
Also: Well-known for his drugs use and convictions for the same, he now says that he occasionally drinks alcohol and consumes hashish and cannabis
Link with the area: He lived there in the 1960s where he wrote (I Can't Get No) Satisfaction

Jubilee Line

Baker Street: Gerry Rafferty

Birth Name: Gerald Rafferty
Born: 16 April 1947. Died: 4 January 20111
Best known as: Singer-songwriter, musician and record producer well-known for his hit song Baker Street
Also: With band Stealers Wheel he produced Stuck In The Middle With You
Link with the area: His song about Baker Street

Jubilee Line

Simon Ghiwas

Westminster: Andrew Graham-Dixon

Birth Name: Andrew Michael Graham-Dixon
Born: 26 December 1960
Best known as: Art historian and broadcaster
Also: He presented A History of British Art (1996) which was nominated for BAFTA and RTS awards; Italy Unpacked with Italian chef Giorgio Locatelli and was a regular on The Culture Show
Link with the area: He went to Westminster School

Jubilee Line

Southwark: Siouxsie Sioux

Birth Name: Susan Janet Ballion
Born: 27 May 1957
Best known as: Singer-songwriter, musician and record producer with her band Siouxsie and the Banshees
Also: They had several top 20 singles including Hong Kong Garden and Kiss Them For Me
Link with the area: She was born in Guy's Hospital in Southwark

Jubilee Line

Bermondsey: Arthur Smith

Birth Name: Brian Arthur John Smith
Born: 27 November 1954
Best known as: Comedian, presenter and writer
Also: In addition to stand-up comedy, he has performed musical comedy shows such as Arthur Smith Sings Leonard Cohen and is a radio presenter on Radio 4 for Excess Baggage and Loose Ends
Link with the area: He was born there

150

Jubilee Line

Canada Water: Danny Baker

Birth Name: Danny Baker
Born: 22 June 1957
Best known as: Comedy writer and broadcaster
Also: Presented Win, Lose or Draw and Pets Win Prizes on television and various
radio shows on Radio London, Radio1, Radio London, Talk Radio and Virgin Radio
Link with the area: He grew up near there

Jubilee Line

Canary Wharf: Robert DeNiro

Birth Name: Robert Anthony De Niro Jr
Born: August 17 1943
Best known as: Actor, producer and director, famous for appearing in Taxi Driver and The Godfather Part II
Also: Particularly well-known for his collaborations with Martin Scorsese, he won an Oscar for Best Supporting Actor in Godfather Part II (1974) and Best Actor for Raging Bull (1980)
Link with the area: He used to have an apartment in the area

Jubilee Line

North Greenwich: Henry VIII

Birth Name: Henry Tudor
Born: 28 June 1491. Died: 28 January 1547
Best known as: King of England
Also: Made himself Supreme head of the Church of England and dissolved the monasteries after disagreeing with Pope Clement VII about the annulment of his marriage to Catherine of Aragon
Link with the area: He was born in Greenwich Palace, now the site of the Old Royal Naval College

Jubilee Line

Canning Town: Charles Canning

Birth Name: Charles Canning
Born: 14 december 1812. Died: 17 June 1862
Best known as: Politician and Statesman
Also: He became Governor-General of India during the Indian Rebellion of 1857 for which he was rewarded with an Earldom
Link with the area: It is named after him

Jubilee Line

West Ham: Martin Peters

Birth Name: Martin Stanford Peters
Born: 8 November 1943. Died: 21 December 2019
Best known as: Professional footballer
Also: He scored the second of England's four goals at the World Cup in 1966
against Germany as well as playing for West Ham United
Link with the area: It was his first professional club and his ashes are interred at
West Ham United's stadium

Metropolitan Line

Amersham: Tim Rice

Birth Name: Timothy Miles Bindon Rice
Born: 10 November 1944
Best known as: Lyricist and author, collaborator with Andrew Lloyd Webber
Also: Shows include Joseph and the Amazing Technicolour Dreamcoat, Jesus Christ Superstar and Evita. He also collaborated with Bjorn Ulvaeus and Benny Andersson on Chess and with Disney on Aladdin and The Lion King amongst many others.
Link with the area: He was born there

Metropolitan Line

Chesham: Aneurin Bevan

Birth Name: Aneurin "Nye" Bevan
Born: 15 November 1897. Died: 6 July 1960
Best known as: Welsh Labour Politician who helped to establish the National Health Service
Also: He was noted orator and Winston Churchill commented that he was "one of the few members that I will sit still and listen to"
Link with the area: He lived there

Metropolitan Line

Chalfont & Latimer: Ozzy Osbourne

Birth Name: John Michael "Ozzy" Osbourne
Born: 3 December 1948
Best known as: Singer-Songwriter with rock band Black Sabbath with songs such as
Diary of a Madman and Over The Mountain
Also: Became a television personality through he reality series The Osbournes
Link with the area: He used to live there

158

Metropolitan Line

Chorleywood: Glen Matlock

Birth Name: Glen Matlock
Born: 27 August 1956
Best known as: Bass guitarist of the Sex Pistols
Also: Went on to form his own bands Rich Kids, Vicious White Kids and Glen Matlock & The Philistines
Link with the area: Went to St Clement Danes School in Chorleywood

Metropolitan Line

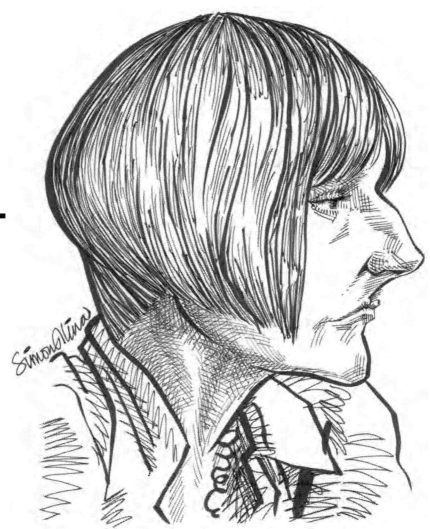

Rickmansworth: Mary Portas

Birth Name: Mary Newton
Born: 28 May 1960
Best known as: Retail consultant and broadcaster
Also: From being a window dresser in Harrods to becoming a board member of
Harvey Nichols she went to present several television programmes about the retail
scene including Mary Queen of Shops and What Britain Buys
Link with the area: She went to school there

Metropolitan Line

Watford: Michael Rosen

Birth Name: Michael Wayne Rosen
Born: 7 May 1946
Best known as: Children's author and poet
Also: He has written 140 books and was Children's Laureate from 2007 to 2009.
We're Going On A Bear Hunt won the Smarties Book Prize in 1989. In 2021 he
released the book Many Different Kinds of Love: A Story of Life, Death and the
NHS, about his experience being hospitalised with COVID-19
Link with the area: He went to Watford Grammar School

Metropolitan Line

Croxley: Fred Housego

Birth Name: Fred Housego
Born: 25 October 1944
Best known as: Taxi driver who became a TV and radio presenter after winning the BBC quiz show Mastermind
Also: Most of his broadcasting career has been on radio, particularly as host of an all-night phone-in show on LBC during the 1990s.
Link with the area: He has lived there

Metropolitan Line

Moor Park: Martin Rowson

Birth Name: Martin Rowson
Born: 15 February 1959
Best known as: Cartoonist on The Guardian newspaper
Also: Produced graphic adaptations of The Waste Land and Tristram Shandy
Link with the area: He went to Merchant Taylor's public school in Moor Park

Metropolitan Line

Northwood: Derek Jarman

Birth Name: Michael Derek Elworthy Jarman
Born: 31 January 1942. Died: 19 February 1994
Best known as: Film director, author and gay rights activist
Also: Films included Sebastiane (1976), Caravaggio (1986) and Blue (1993).
Outspoken about homosexuality and gay rights, he died of an AIDS-related illness
Link with the area: He was born in the Royal Victoria Nursing Home there

Metropolitan Line

Northwood Hills: Audley Harrison

Birth Name: Audley Hugh Harrison
Born: 26 October 1971
Best known as: Professional boxer
Also: He won the Super Heavyweight Gold Medal for Great Britain at the 2000
Olympics in Sydney
Link with the area: He went to school there

Metropolitan Line

Pinner: Elton John

Birth Name: Reginald Kenneth Dwight
Born: 25 March 1947
Best known as: Singer, pianist and composer who co-wrote Candle In The Wind and Rocketman
Also: Collaborating with lyricist Bernie Taupin, he has sold over 300 million records and he won the Academy Award for Best Original Song for Can You Feel the Love Tonight from The Lion King
Link with the area: He was raised there

Metropolitan Line

North Harrow: Courtney Pine

Birth Name: Courtney Pine
Born: 18 March 1964
Best known as: Jazz musician playing saxophone alongside singers such as Elkie
Brooks (Too Much to Lose) and Micah Paris (Like Dreamers Do)
Also: Founded the black British big band the Jazz Warriors
Link with the area: He lives there

Metropolitan Line

Ickenham: Sue Cook

Birth Name: Susan Lorraine Thomas
Born: 30 March 1949
Best known as: Television presenter and author
Also: Best-known for presenting Crimewatch with Nick Ross and she is often referenced "as a friend" of Alan Partridge in Steve Coogan's I'm Alan Partridge
Link with the area: She used to live there

Metropolitan Line

West Harrow: Tim Dooley

Birth Name: Tim Dooley
Born: 1951
Best known as: Poet
Also: Has taught in schools and Further Education and is reviews and features
editor of Poetry London
Link with the area: He lives there

Metropolitan Line

Harrow-on-the-Hill: Ginger Baker

Birth Name: Peter Edward "Ginger" Baker
Born: 19 August 1939. Died: 6 October 2019
Best known as: Drummer for the rock band Cream
Also: He went to join Blind Faith and then to form his own band Ginger Baker's Air Force, described as a jazz-rock fusion supergroup including fellow musicians Denny Laine and Steve Winwood
Link with the area: He used to live there

Metropolitan Line

Northwick Park: Michael Portillo

Birth Name: Michael Denzil Xavier Portillo
Born: 26 May 1953
Best known as: Journalist, broadcaster and former politician
Also: His television shows include Great British Railway Journeys and Great Continental Railway Journeys. As a boy, he appeared in a television commercial for Ribena
Link with the area: He was educated at nearby Harrow County School

Metropolitan Line

Preston Road: Jim Slater

Birth Name: James Derrick Slater
Born: 13 March 1929. Died: 18 November 2015
Best known as: Accountant and investor, the founder of investment bank
Slater Walker
Also: Slater Walker collapsed in the banking crisis of 1973-75. He donated $125k to
fund the 1972 World Chess Championship between Bobby Fischer and Boris Spassky
Link with the area: He had a home in the area

Northern Line

High Barnet: Emma Bunton

Birth Name: Emma Lee Bunton
Born: 21 January 1976, Finchley
Best known as: Singer "Baby Spice" in the 1990s girl group Spice Girls which sold 85 million records worldwide to become the best-selling female group of all time.
Also: A radio and television presenter, singer, songwriter and actress
Link with area: She attended Underhill School in High Barnet and moved back to the area in 2006

Northern Line

Totteridge and Whetstone: Arsène Wenger

Birth Name: Arsène Charles Ernest Wenger OBE
Born: 22 October 1949, Strasbourg, France
Best known as: Arsenal's longest-serving and most successful manager (from 1996 to 2018)
Also: He is currently FIFA's Chief of Global Football Development.
Link with area: Can be seen riding his bike around this exclusive suburb where he now lives

Woodside Park: Spike Milligan

Birth Name:Terence Alan "Spike" Milligan KBE
Born: 16 April 1918, Ahmednagar, India. Died: 27 February 2002, Rye
Best known as: The eccentric creator of The Goon Show (with Michael Bentine)
Also: Best-selling author, (Hitler, My Part in His Downfall), poet, actor, playwright
and soldier. Voted the funniest comedian of the last millennium in a BBC
online vote
Link with area: Lived at 127 Holden Road (site now marked with a blue plaque
placed in 2004) President and Patron of the Finchley Society

Northern Line

Northern Line

West Finchley: John Bercow

Birth Name: John Simon Bercow
Born: 19 January 1963
Best known as: Former speaker of the House of Commons from 2009 to 2019
Also: Served as a Member of Parliament for Buckingham between 1997 and 2019.
Link with area: Attended Finchley Manor Hill Comprehensive School

Northern Line

Finchley Central:Terry-Thomas

Birth Name: Thomas Terry Hoar Stevens
Born: 10 July 1911. Died: 8 January 1990
Best known as: an eccentric gap-toothed comedian and character actor. Films include I'm Alright Jack and School for Scoundrels
Also: Changed his name after being continually asked if he was related to Ellen Terry the actress (the hyphen in his name was to represent the gap in his teeth.)
Link with area: Born in in Lichfield Grove, Finchley

Northern Line

Mill Hill East: Patrick McGoohan

Birth Name: Patrick Joseph McGoohan
Born: 19 March 1928. Died: 13 January 2009
Best known as: a gravelly-voiced TV star in the 1950s to 1960s, starring as Number 6 in the surreal science fiction series, The Prisoner (1967).
Also: Starred in Danger Man (1960), Secret Agent (1964), and Rafferty (1977).
Link with the area: At the height of his fame in The Prisoner he lived in a house off the Ridgeway

Northern Line

East Finchley: Jerry Springer

Birth Name: Gerald Norman Springer
Born: February 13 1944
Best known as: Presenter of the Jerry Springer Show
Also: known as a broadcaster, journalist, actor, producer and former lawyer
and politician
Link with the area: Jerry Springer was born in the underground tunnel between
East Finchley and Highgate Station during an air raid in the Blitz of the Second
World War

179

Northern Line

Highgate: Karl Marx

Birth Name:: Karl Heinrich Marx
Born: 5 May 1818. Died: 14 March 1883
Best known as: Philosopher, economist, historian and political theorist
Also: Well-known for his Communist Manifesto and Das Kapital stating that human societies develop through class conflict; a theory becoming known as Marxism. he is one of the most influential figures in history but his work is both lauded and criticised. Many political parties worldwide have modified and adapted his ideas and he is seen as one of the priciple architects of modern social science
Link with the area: Karl Marx is buried in Highgate Cemetery. His tomb is a magnet for both his supporters and his detractors

Northern Line

Archway: Ray Davies

Birth Name: Raymond Douglas Davies
Born: 21 June 1944
Best known as: The lead singer, rhythm guitarist and main songwriter for the Kinks whose hits include You Really Got Me and Lola
Also: He has acted, directed and produced shows for theatre and television.
Link with the area: Early on in his career, The Kinks regularly played at the 'Archway Tavern', depicted on the cover artwork of their 1971 album, Muswell Hillbillies

Northern Line

Tufnell Park: Damian Lewis

Birth Name:: Damian Watcyn Lewis OBE
Born: 11 February 1971
Best known as: An actor, presenter, and producer.
Also: Starred in Band of Brothers, Homeland, Night Manager and Wolf Hall.
Link with the area: He lives in Tufnell Park having bought his friend Hugh Laurie's old house

Northern Line

Kentish Town: Eddy Grant

Birth Name:: Edmond Montague Grant
Born: 5 March 1948
Best known as: A singer-songwriter and musician
Also: He was a founding member of The Equals who had a number one hit with
Baby Come Back and he pioneered the genre Ringbang
Link with the area: He spent his formative years here attending Acland Burghley,
one of the country's leading state schools for art, music, and drama

Northern Line

Camden Town: Dylan Thomas

Birth Name: Dylan Marlais Thomas
Born: 27 October 1914. Died: 9 November 1953
Best known as: A tempestuous Welsh poet and writer
Also: His works include the poems Do not go gentle into that good night and And
death shall have no dominion; the play, Under Milk Wood; and stories and radio
broadcasts such as A Child's Christmas in Wales and Portrait of the Artist as a
Young Dog
Link with the area: He lived at 54 Delancey Street, Camden Town from 1951-1952

Northern Line

Mornington Crescent: Walter Sickert

Birth Name: Walter Richard Sickert
Born: 31 May 1860. Died: 22 January 1942
Best known as: a painter and printmaker
Also: He was a member of the Camden Town Group of Post-Impressionist artists in early 20th-century London and an important influence on avant-garde art in the mid- and late 20th century. Some people, disturbed by the macabre nature of some of his work have suggested that he might have been Jack the Ripper.
Link with the area: His studio was in a sparse Mornington Crescent boarding house where he used local prostitutes as models. One of his works is Mornington Crescent Nude, c1907 (Fitzwilliam Museum, Cambridge)

Northern Line

Euston: Virginia Woolf

Birth Name: Adeline Virginia Woolf
Born: 25 January 1882. Died: 28 March 1941
Best known as: One of the more important modernist 20th century authors.
Also: She pioneered the use of stream of consciousness as a narrative. Her works include Mrs Dalloway (1925), To the Lighthouse (1927), Orlando: A Biography (1928) and The Waves (1931)
Link with the area: Virginia lived at 29 Fitzroy Square with her brother Adrian from 1907 hosting informal gatherings with friends– among them Lytton Strachey, Roger Fry, EM Forster and John Maynard Keynes who would later become collectively known as the Bloomsbury Group. George Bernard Shaw was a previous tenant at number 29

Northern Line

Warren Street: George Bernard Shaw

Birth Name: George Bernard Shaw
Born: 26 July 1856. Died: 2 November 1950
Best known as: An Irish playwright
Also: He was also a literary critic, polemicist and a prominent socialist. His most successful work, Pygmalion, was adapted as the musical My Fair Lady. He won the Nobel Prize for Literature in 1925
Link with the area: He lived at 29 Fitzroy Square, London from 1887 TO 1898. He also named the protagonist in his play Mrs Warren's Profession after a scandal involving the radical MP Sir Charles Dilke who was accused of conducting an adulterous affair in a rented room on Warren Street

Northern Line

Goodge Street: Charles Laughton

Birth Name: Charles Laughton
Born: 1 July 1899, Died: 15 December 1962
Best known as: a stage and film actor and director, playing The Hunchback of
Notre Dame and Henry VIII
Also: He directed the acclaimed The Night of the Hunter and Daniel Day-Lewis has
said "He was probably the greatest film actor who came from that period of time."
Link with the area: He lived with his wife, Bride of Frankenstein actress Elsa
Lanchester, at 15 Percy Street from 1928-1931

Northern Line

Tottenham Court Road: Roger Waters

Birth Name: George Roger Waters
Born: 6 September 1943
Best known as: co-founder of progressive rock band Pink Floyd who had best selling albums Dark Side of the Moon and The Wall
Also: Known for his pro-Palestine sentiments and activism
Link with the area: His career with Pink Floyd was launched when they had a residency at The UFO club in the basement of 31 Tottenham Court Road, under the Gala Berkeley Cinema

Northern Line

Leicester Square: William Hogarth

Birth Name: William Hogarth
Born: 10 November. Died: 26 October 1764
Best known as: A political satirical cartoonist. Produced the A Harlot's Progress, A Rake's Progress and Marriage A-la-Mode series.
Also: A painter and printmaker
Link with the area: Lived with his wife in a house which stood at the south-eastern corner of Leicester Fields (now Leicester Square) from 1733 until his death in 1764

Northern Line

Charing Cross: Rudyard Kipling

Birth Name: Joseph Rudyard Kipling
Born: 30 December 1865. Died: 18 January 1936
Best known for: His children's stories including The Jungle Book (1894) and Just So Stories (1902).
Also: For his stories and poems of British soldiers in India including Mandalay, Gunga Din and If—.
Link with the area: From 1889 to 1891, Rudyard Kipling lived at number 4, Villiers Street (later renamed Kipling House) which is marked with a blue plaque

Northern Line

Embankment: Richard Harris

Birth Name: Richard John Harris
Born: 1 October 1930. Died: 25 October 2002
Best known as: A hell-raising Irish actor and singer
Also: He was nominated for the Academy Award for Best Actor in This Sporting
Life (1963) and played King Arthur in the 1967 film Camelot and again in the 1981
stage musical revival
Link with the area: He used to enjoy a drink or two at The Coal Hole on The Strand

Northern Line

Waterloo: Duke of Wellington

Birth Name: Arthur Wellesley
Born: 1 May 1769. Died: 14 September 1852
Best known: For commanding the British, German, Dutch and Belgian troops that defeated Napoleon Bonaparte at the battle of Waterloo in 1815. one of the leading military
Also: Was one of the major political figures of 19th-century Britain, he was prime minister twice and Leader of the House of Lords from 1841–1846)
Link with the area: The Station was named in honour of the famous battle as was the bridge and many pubs!

Northern Line

Edgware: Fenella Fielding

Birth Name: Fenella Marion Feldman
Born: 17 November 1927. Died: 11 September 2018
Best known for: Playing seductive and husky voiced femmes fatales in 1950s and 1960s Carry On and Doctor films.
Also: She was often referred to as "England's first lady of the double entendre".
Link with the area: She attended North London Collegiate School in Edgware.

Northern Line

Burnt Oak: Jack Cohen

Birth Name: Sir John "Jack" Edward Cohen
Born: 6 October 1898. Died: 24 March 1979
Best known As: an English grocer who founded the Tesco supermarket chain.
Also: He was a philanthropist who supported a range of charities in Britain and in Israel, his wife gave her name to the Jewish Care facility, Lady Sarah Cohen House in Friern Barnet, North London
Link with the area: He opened the first Tesco shop in September 1931 in Burnt Oak

Northern Line

Colindale: Claude Grahame-White

Birth Name: Claude Grahame-White
Born: 21 August 1879. Died: 19 August 1959
Best known as: An English pioneer of aviation
Also: He was the first to make a night flight, during the Daily Mail-sponsored 1910
London to Manchester air race
Link with the area: He established the Flying School at Hendon Aerodrome near
Colindale in 1911

Northern Line

Hendon Central: Henry Cooper

Name: Sir Henry Cooper OBE KSG
Born: 3 May 1934. Died: 1 May 2011
Best known as: A British heavyweight boxer with an unmatched British record – winner of 40 of his 55 contests, 27 by knockout, one drawn, in a 17-year career from 1954 to 1971
Also: For the 1963 fight with Muhammad Ali who was "saved by the bell" and went on to win after Henry felled him with 'Enry's 'Ammer. The two remained friends until Henry's death
Link with the area: He lived at 36 Brampton Grove Hendon from 1979, regularly attending Our Lady of Dolours Church

Northern Line

Brent Cross: Vanessa Feltz

Birth Name: Vanessa Jane Feltz
Born: 21 February 1962, Islington, London
Best known as: An English television personality, broadcaster, and journalist.
Also: For appearing in various television shows, including Vanessa, The Big
Breakfast, The Vanessa Show, Celebrity Big Brother, The Wright Stuff, This
Morning, and Strictly Come Dancing
Link with the area: She was a constant visitor to Brent Cross Shopping Centre from
its opening in 1976 when she was 14 years old and was invited to the celebrations
of it 40th anniversary

Northern Line

Golders Green: Helena Bonham-Carter

Birth Name: Helena Bonham Carter
Born: 26 May 1966
Best known as: An English actress in films such as A Room With A View, The King's Speech and Harry Potter and the Deathly Hallows. She has been awarded a British Academy Film Award, two Screen Actors Guild Awards, and nominations for two Academy Awards, eight Golden Globes, four Primetime Emmy Awards and three British Academy Television Awards
Also: Her relationships with Kenneth Branagh (1994–1999) and Tim Burton (2001–2014)
Link with the area: She was born and brought up in Golders Green and lived with her parents until she was 30 when she moved a few miles away to Hampstead

Northern Line

Hampstead: Ricky Gervais

Birth Name: Ricky Dene Gervais
Born: 25 June 1961
Best known as: An English comedian, actor, writer and creator of the television mockumentary sitcom The Office
Also: He wrote and created Extras, Life's Too Short, An Idiot Abroad, Derek and After Life
Link with the area: He lives in the area and enjoys walks on Hampstead Heath

Northern Line

Belsize Park: Martin Freeman

Birth Name: Martin John Christopher Freeman
Born: 8 September 1971
Best known as: An English actor. He has won an Emmy Award, a BAFTA Award and a Screen Actors Guild Award, and has been nominated for a Golden Globe Award
Also: For playing Tim Canterbury in The Office, Dr Watson in Sherlock and Bilbo Baggins in The Hobbit
Link with the area: Following his split from Sherlock costar actress Amanda Abbington he bought a luxury mansion in Belsize Park

Northern Line

Chalk Farm: Sienna Miller

Birth Name: Sienna Rose Diana Miller
Born: 28 December 1981
Best known as: A British-American actress who made her acting breakthrough in the 2004 films Layer Cake and Alfie
Also: She began her career as a photography model in Italian Vogue and posing topless for the 2003 Pirelli calendar and dated Jude Law
Link with the area: Along with Jude Law and Sadie Frost she used to be one of the 'Camden set' of writers, artists and actors living in this area

Northern Line

King's Cross St Pancras: Sir John Betjeman

Birth Name: John Betjemann
Born: 28 August 1906. Died: 19 May 1984
Best known as: Writer, broadcaster and Poet Laureate, 1972 - 1984
Also: He wrote the book London's Historic Railway Stations. He was a founding member of The Victorian Society and well-known as a passionate defender of Victorian architecture
Link with the area: He helped to save St Pancras station from demolition

Northern Line

Angel: Boris Johnson

Birth Name: Alexander Boris de Pfeffel Johnson
Born: 19 June 1964
Best known as: A British politician, author, and journalist
Also: As the Prime Minister of the United Kingdom who had to finalize Brexit and deal with the Covid crisis. His books include The Churchill Factor and Johnson's Life of London
Link with the area: He lived in the area with his wife, Marina Wheeler QC. His house was sold in 2019

Old Street: William Blake

Birth Name: William Blake
Born: 28 November, 1757 in Soho, London
Died: 12 August 1827 in Charing Cross , London
Best known as: Poet who wrote Jerusalem and Tyger, painter and printmaker
Also: A visionary mystic regarded as a seminal figure in the history of the poetry and visual art of the romantic age
Link with the area: He is buried in Bunhill Fields near Old Street station

Northern Line

Moorgate: John Keats

Birth Name: John Keats
Born: 31 October 1795. Died: 23 February 1821
Best known as: One of the major Romantic poets along with Lord Byron and Percy Bysshe Shelley. His many well-known works include Ode to a Nightingale and Ode to Autumn
Also: His works were only in publication for four years before his death from tuberculosis at the age of 25
Link with the area: He is believed to have been born in The Swan and Hoop Livery Stables, just north of the old London Wall. The current building now houses the Keats at the Globe Bar

Northern Line

Bank: Thomas Rowlandson

Birth Name: Thomas Rowlandson
Born: 14 July 1756. Died: 22 April 1827
Best known as: An Georgian artist and caricaturist, noted for his political satire and social observation
Also: He produced highly explicit erotica for a private clientele which wasn't made public at the time
Link with the area: Born in the financial centre of London, he designed and etched a picture of The Great Hall of the Bank of England on February 1, 1808

Northern Line

London Bridge: George Orwell

Birth Name: Eric Arthur Blair
Born: 25 June 1903. Died: 21 January 1950
Best known as: An English novelist, essayist, journalist and critic
Also: For his opposition to totalitarianism and support of democratic socialism as
shown in his novels Animal Farm (1945) and Nineteen Eighty-Four (1949).
Link with the area: In order to research his Down and Out in Paris and London
(1933) he stayed in a doss-house in Tooley Street, London Bridge from 19th
September to 8th October, 1931

Northern Line

Borough: David Bomberg

Birth Name: David Garshen Bomberg
Born: 5 December 1890. Died: 19 August 1957
Best known as: Painter of complex geometric compositions
Also: His work became more figurative during the 1920s
Link with the area: He taught at Borough Polytechnic (now London South Bank
University) where his pupils included Frank Auerbach and Leon Kossof

Northern Line

Elephant and Castle: Michael Caine

Birth Name: Maurice Joseph Micklewhite Jr
Born: 14 March 1933
Best known as: Actor who has appeared in more than 130 films winning two
Academy Awards for best supporting actor. He received the best actor award from
the BAFTAs and the Golden Globes for Educating Rita. Two other well-known
Michael Caine films are The Italian Job and The Ipcress File
Also: Well-known for his South London accent and quotes such as "You're only
supposed to blow the bloody doors off"
Link with the area: His family moved to Kennington when he was small

Northern Line

Kennington: Florence Welch

Birth Name: Florence Leontine Mary Welch
Born: 28 August 1986
Best known as: Singer/songwriter in rock band Florence and the Machine with their hit Dog Days are Over
Also: Has won many awards including the Ivor Novello Award for International Achievement and the Silver Clef Award for Best Female
Link with the area: She was brought up in nearby camberwell and moved to a house in Kennington

Northern Line

Nine Elms: Joanna Lumley

Birth Name: Joanna Lamond Lumley
Born: 1 May 1946
Best known as: Actress, former model and activist
Also: Best known for TV roles in Absolutely Fabulous (as Patsy), The New Avengers (Purdey) and Sapphire and Steel
Link with the area: It is said that she shops in the Nine Elms area

Northern Line

Battersea Power Station: Gordon Ramsay

Birth Name: Gordon James Ramsay
Born: 8 November 1966
Best known as: Chef, restaurateur and television personality in shows such as
Hell's Kitchen
Also: Known for his volatile manner and frequent colourful language
Link with the area: Owns a restaurant near Battersea Power Station called
Street Pizza

Northern Line

Oval: Sir Paul Getty

Birth Name: Eugene Paul Getty
Born: 7 September 1932. Died: 17 April 2003
Best known as: Philanthropist and book collector and the third of five sons to J. Paul Getty
Also: His son, Jon Paul Getty III was kidnapped and held to ransom in Italy. He was awarded a knighthood for his services to cricket, Art and to the Conservative party
Link with the area: He constructed a replica of the Oval cricket ground within his estate in Wormsley, Buckinghamshire

Northern Line

Stockwell: Will Self

Birth Name: William Woodard Self
Born: 26 September 1961
Best known as: Author, journalist and broadcaster
Also: Has won the Geoffrey Faber Memorial Prize for the Quantity Theory of Insanity and his recent novel Umbrella was shortlisted for the Man Booker prize. Whilst covering the election campaign of John Major in 1997, Self was caught using heroin on the Prime Minister's jet and was fired. He collects typewriters
Link with the area: Self has a house in Stockwell

Northern Line

Clapham North: Margot Robbie

Birth Name: Margot Elise Robbie
Born: 2 July 1990
Best known as: Australian actress who starred in I, Tonya and who received two Academy Award nominations and five British Academy film Award nominations
Also: She came to attention in the Australian TV soap Neighbours and is a vocal supporter human rights, gender equality and LCBT rights
Link with the area: It is said that Margot Robbie used to go to the nightclub Infernos in Clapham

Northern Line

Clapham Common: Miriam Margolyes

Birth Name: Miriam Margolyes
Born: 18 May 1941
Best known as: Actress who won the British Academy Film Award for Best
Supporting Actress in The Age of Innocence. Currently a regular character in the
TV series Call the Midwife
Also: She appeared as Professor Pomona Sprout in two Harry Potter films. She is a
Corbyn-supporting Labour Party member
Link with the area: She has a house near Clapham Common

Northern Line

Clapham South: Vanessa Redgrave

Birth Name: Vanessa Redgrave
Born: 30 January 1937
Best known as: Multi-award winning actress and activist. She won the Best Supporting Actress award sat the oscars for her role in Julia
Also: Laurence Olivier announced her birth during a performance of Hamlet at the Old Vic. Her father, Sir Michael Redgrave was playing Laertes and Olivier said "Laertes has had a daughter", adding "A great actress has been born this night."
Link with the area: Redgrave has had a home there for years

Balham: Jimmy Hill

Birth Name: James William Thomas Hill
Born: 22 July 1928. Died: 19 December 2015
Best known as: Footballer and television personality
Also: Mainly known as presenter of BBC's Match of the Day during which he was present when the Hillsborough disaster happened in 1989
Link with the area: Jimmy Hill was born in Balham

Northern Line

Tooting Bec: St. Anselm

Birth Name: Anselmo d'Aosta
Born: 1033 or 1034. Died: 1109
Best known as: Benedictine monk, Abbot and philosopher who was Archbishop of Canterbury from 1093 to 1109
Also: He was canonised as a saint after his death and his feast day is 21 April
Link with the area: Anselm established a small priory in the area

Northern Line

Tooting Broadway: Sadiq Khan

Birth Name: Sadiq Aman Khan
Born: 8 October 1970
Best known as: Labour politician and Mayor of London
Also: His father was a London bus driver. As Mayor of London he has been instrumental in introducing preventing fare rises in "single fares" on the buses and the tube
Link with the area: Sadiq Khan was born in St George's Hospital in Tooting

Northern Line

Colliers Wood: St. Thomas Becket

Birth Name: Thomas Becket
Born: 21 December 1119 or 1120. Died: 29 December 1170
Best known as: Archbishop of Canterbury from 1162 until 1170 when he was murdered in the Cathedral due to a possible misundertstood utterance by King Henry II
Also: King Henry II is alleged to have uttered "Who will rid me of this turbulent priest?" Which was overheard and taken to be a command
Link with the area: Merton Priory was situated in the area and St. Thomas Becket is said to have studied there

Northern Line

South Wimbledon: Oliver Reed

Birth Name: Robert Oliver Reed
Born: 13 February 1938. Died: 2 May 1999
Best known as: Actor with a macho attitude and a hell-raising lifestyle whose films included The Devils and Women in Love
Also: A little known fact is that Oliver Reed was considered for the role of James Bond after Sean Connery left the franchise. "One of the great missed opportunities of post-war British movie history" said one commentator
Link with the area: A Wimbledon resident, Oliver Reed would often do an infamous pub crawl known as the Wimbledon Eight consisting of drinking a pint in fifteen minutes at each of the eight pubs

Northern Line

Morden: Admiral Mariot Arbuthnot

Birth Name: Mariot Arbuthnot
Born: 1711. Died: 31 January 1794
Best known as: British Admiral commanding the Royal Navy during the American War of independence
Also: Contemporary colleagues were less than impressed by his rudimentary grasp of Naval discipline and tactics
Link with the area: He lived there in his latter years

Cockfosters: Bernie Winters

Birth Name: Bernard Weinstein
Born: 6 September 1930. Died: 4 May 1991
Best known as: A comedian in a double act with his brother Mike in the 1970s and 80s
Also: Having fallen out with his brother, Bernie formed a new double act with his St Bernard dog, Schnorbitz
Link with area: Bernie was always a North London man (despite having written "Give Me A Cockney Song") and he lived in Cockfosters for some time

225

Piccadilly Line

Oakwood: Cliff Richard

Birth Name: Harry Rodger Webb
Born: 14 October 1940
Best known as: An English pop singer whose career dates from the late 1950s to the present day. He is the third-top-selling artist in UK Singles Chart history, after the Beatles and Elvis Presley. His hits include Devil Woman and Congratulations which came second in the 1968 Eurovision Song Contest
Also: For his firm adherence to Christianity and generous donations to charity
Link with area: Cliff is a long-term supporter of Chickenshed, the inclusive theatre company near Oakwood

Piccadilly Line

Southgate: Amy Winehouse

Birth Name: Amy Jade Winehouse
Born: 14 September 1983. Died: 23 July 2011
Best known as: A British singer and songwriter with deep, expressive contralto vocals and an eclectic mix of musical genres, including soul, rhythm and blues and jazz. A big hit was Back to Black
Also: Amy was plagued by drug and alcohol addiction and died of alcohol poisoning at the age of 27
Link with area: Amy grew up in Osidge Lane, Southgate and attended Osidge Primary School

Piccadilly Line

Arnos Grove: Charles Holden

Birth Name: Charles Henry Holden
Born: 12 May 1875. Died: 1 May 1960
Best known as: An architect whose ground-breaking station designs are regarded as some of the finest examples of British commercial architecture
Also: He created many war cemeteries in Belgium and northern France for the Imperial War Graves Commission
Link with area: Arnos Grove Underground Station is considered to be one of Holden's finest station designs

Bounds Green: Dan Gillespie Sells

Birth Name: Daniel Giles Gillespie Sells
Born: 20 September 1978
Best known as: An English singer-songwriter and guitarist, and the lead vocalist and frontman for the rock group The Feeling (Fill My Little World)
Also: Dan attended The Ashmole School in London along with fellow students Amy Winehouse and Rachel Stevens (S Club 7)
Link with area: Dan grew up in Bounds Green and some members of The Feeling still live in the area. The title of the Feeling's first album, Twelve Stops and Home, refers to the journey Gillespie used to make home to Bounds Green from Leicester Square

Piccadilly Line

Wood Green: Trevor Phillips

Birth Name: Mark Trevor Phillips
Born: 31 December 1953
Best known as: A British writer, broadcaster and former Labour politician
Also: He was appointed head of the Commission for Racial Equality (CRE) by Prime Minister Tony Blair in 2003 and was the chairman of the Equality and Human Rights Commission (EHRC) from 2007 to 2012
Link with area: Trevor spent his childhood partly in British Guiana, and partly in Wood Green attending Wood Green County Grammar School in White Hart Lane

Piccadilly Line

Turnpike Lane: Mark Knopfler

Birth Name: Mark Freuder Knopfler
Born: 12 August 1949, Glasgow, Scotland
Best known as: The British lead guitarist, singer and songwriter of the rock band
Dire Straits (Sultans of Swing, Money For Nothing)
Also: Knopfler is left-handed, but plays the guitar right-handed
Link with area: Mark Knopfler's song Junkie Doll features the lyrics :
"Turnpike Lane, Turnpike Lane You spiked my arm. But you missed the vein."

Piccadilly Line

Manor House: Richard Desmond

Birth Name: Richard Clive Desmond
Born: 8 December 1951
Best known as: A billionaire British publisher, businessman and former pornographer, publishing the Daily Express and Daily Star
Also: In 2020, Desmond persuaded the Secretary of State for Housing, Communities and Local Government Robert Jenrick to approve a housing development for Desmond's company saving the company £40 million. This ruling was later overturned
Link with area: When he was 13, Desmond worked in the cloakroom of the Manor House pub, quickly realising that if he put two coats on a single hanger he could pocket an extra sixpence. He jokingly says that if he became a member of the House of Lords he could be known as "Lord Desmond of Manor House"

Piccadilly Line

Arsenal: Mesut Özil

Birth Name: Mesut Özil
Born: 15 October 1988
Best known as: A German professional footballer who plays as an attacking midfielder for Süper Lig club Fenerbahçe. Özil is known for his technical skills, creativity, passing skills, and vision. He can also play as a wide midfielder
Also: As the son of Turkish immigrants Özil was eligible to play for either Turkey or Germany. It was only after considerable deliberation that he decided to play for the country of his birth
Link with area: Özil played for Arsenal football club from 2013–2021, making 184 appearances and scoring 33 goals

Piccadilly Line

Holloway Road: Joe Meek

Birth Name: Robert George Meek. Also known as Robert Duke and Peter Jacobs
Born 5 April 1929. Died 3 February 1967
Best known as: One of the most influentialrecord producers of all time. His
masterpiece, Telstar, was a number one in the UK, and it became the first single by
a British group to hit number one in the United States
Also: His success was shortlived and depression and mental problems ended in
him murdering his landlady and committing suicide
Link with area: Between 1961 and 1967, he rented the accommodation above 304
Holloway Road setting up a makeshift but innovative studio and the independent
label RGM Records (from Joe's birth name, Robert George Meek)

Piccadilly Line

Caledonian Road: Emily Thornberry

Birth Name: Emily Anne Thornberry
Born: 27 July 1960
Best known as: Labour politician, formerly serving as Shadow Attorney General and Shadow Secretary of State for Foreign and Commonwealth Affairs
Also: In 2006, Thornberry won the ePolitix Award for Environment Champion of the Year and In 2008, she supported a change in the law to allow single women and lesbian couples to seek in vitro fertilisation treatment. Her husband is High Court judge Sir Christopher Nugee but Thornberry does not use the title Lady Nugee
Link with area: She lives nearby

Piccadilly Line

Russell Square: Charles Dickens

Birth Name: Charles John Huffam Dickens
Born: 7 February 1812. Died: 9 June 1870
Best known as: English writer an social critic, author of Oliver Twist, Great Expectations and many others
Also: He wanted to be buried at Rochester Cathedral "in an inexpensive, unostentatious and strictly private manner" but was laid to rest in Poets Corner at Westminster Abbey
Link with area: He lived at 48 Doughty Street, now the home of the Charles Dickens Museum

Piccadilly Line

Covent Garden: John Logie Baird

Birth Name: John Logie Baird
Born: 13 August 1888. Died: 14 June 1946
Best known as: Inventor of the television
Also: He was the only deceased subject of television's This Is Your Life, presented by Eamonn Andrews in 1957
Link with area: Shortly after demonstrating television in Soho, he moved to Long Acre in Covent Garden in 1928

Piccadilly Line

Piccadilly Circus: Aleister Crowley

Birth Name: Edward Alexander Crowley
Born: 12 October 1875. Died: 1 December 1947
Best known as: Occultist, magician and painter
Also: He founded the religion of Thelema as a 'prophet' who would guide humanity into the 'Aeon of Horus' in the early twentieth century. He did not consider himself the Satanist that so many considered him to be although he used Satanic imagery such as the "Beast 666" and referring to the Whore of Babylon in his works
Link with area: He used to live in a flat in Jermyn Street

Hyde Park Corner: Fred Astaire

Birth Name: Frederick Austerlitz
Born: 10 May 1899. Died: 22 June 1987
Best known as: Dancer, actor and singer in films such as Top Hat and Funny Face
Also: His awards include an honorary Oscar for "his unique artistry and contribution to musical pictures" in 1950 and being named "Musical Comedy Star of the Century" by Liberty, "The Nostalgia Magazine"
Link with area: He owned a Georgian townhouse nearby

Piccadilly Line

Knightsbridge: Ava Gardner

Birth Name: Ava Lavinia Gardner
Born: 24 December 1922. Died: 25 January 1990
Best known as: Actress and singer in films such as The Life and Times of Judge Roy Bean (1972) and The Hucksters (1947)
Also: She married Mickey Rooney, Artie Shaw andFrank Sinatra
Link with area: She lived in Ennismore Gardens from 1968

240

Piccadilly Line

South Kensington: Benny Hill

Birth Name: Alfred Hawthorne "Benny" Hill
Born: 21 January 1924. Died: 20 April 1992
Best known as: Comedian, singer and writer
Also: Best remembered for The Benny Hill Show full of slapstick, burlesque and
double entendres, he had celebrity fans such as Johnny Carson, Charlie Chaplin
and Michael Jackson
Link with area: He rented an apartment in Queen's Gate for many years

Piccadilly Line

Gloucester Road: Madonna

Birth Name: Madonna Louise Ciccone
Born: 16 August 1958
Best known as: Singer-songwriter (Like a Virgin, Material Girl)
Also: Noted for her continual reinvention with works that include social, political, sexual and religious themes. She has won seven Grammy Awards and twenty MTV Video Music Awards
Link with area: She was, for a time, a regular at Da Mario's, a pizza restaurant there

Piccadilly Line

Earl's Court: Willie Rushton

Birth Name: William George Rushton
Born: 18 August 1937. Died: 11 December 1996
Best known as: Cartoonist, satirist and actor who appeared on satirical television show That Was The Week That Was and contributed to many radio shows
Also: He co-founded the satirical magazine Private Eye. His recreations are listed in Who's Who as "gaining weight, losing weight and parking"
Link with area: He was born in the local Cromwell Hospital

Piccadilly Line

Barons Court: Mahatma Gandhi

Birth Name: Mohandas Karamchand Gandhi
Born: 2 October 1869. Died: 30 January 1948
Best known as: Indian lawyer and anti-colonial nationalist
Also: He employed non-violent resistance to campaign for India's independence
from British rule
Link with area: He lived there while studying law in London

244

Piccadilly Line

Hammersmith: Bill Bailey

Birth Name: Mark Robert Bailey
Born: 13 January 1965
Best known as: Comedian, musician and actor with appearances on Never Mind
The Buzzcocks and in the sitcom Black Books
Also: He plays a range of musical instruments and includes them in his
stand-up acts
Link with area: He lives there

Piccadilly Line

Turnham Green: Peter Brook

Birth Name: Peter Stephen Paul Brook
Born: 21 March 1925
Best known as: Theatre and film directorwho produced Dr Faustus and The Infernal
Machine amongst others
Also: He has won multiple Tony and Emmy Awards, a Laurence Olivier Award
amongst others and has been called "our greatest living theatre director"
Link with area: He was born near there

Acton Town: Lionel Bart

Birth Name: Lionel Bart
Born: 1 August 1930. Died: 3 April 1999
Best known as: Writer and composer of pop music and musicals
Also: He was the sole creator of the musical Oliver! in 1960 and in 1963 won the
the Tony Award for Best Original Score
Link with area: He lived there until his death

Piccadilly Line

South Ealing: Bob Block

Birth Name: Bob Block
Born: 20 July 1921. Died: 17 April 2011
Best known as: Comedy scriptwriter
Also: On radio, he was best known for co-writing Life with the Lyons and on childrens' comedy series on television such as Pardon My Genie and Rentaghost
Link with area: He lived there

Northfields: Dusty Springfield

Birth Name: Mary Isobel Catherine Bernadette O'Brien
Born: 16 April 1939. Died: 2 March 1999
Best known as: Pop singer who had a hit with Son of a Preacher Man
Also: As one of the most successful female performers of the time, she became an
icon of the Sixties with her trademark bouffant/beehive and thick black eyeliner
Link with area: She lived between there and Ealing

Piccadilly Line

Piccadilly Line

Boston Manor: Christopher Clitherow

Birth Name: Christopher Clitherow
Born: 10 January 1578. Died: 11 November 1641
Best known as: Merchant and politician
Also: He was Lord Mayor of London in 1635 and helped in efforts to discover the North West passage
Link with area: He was the third owner of Boston Manor, a house built in 1622

Piccadilly Line

Osterley: Roland Penrose

Birth Name: Roland Algernon Penrose
Born: 14 October 1900. Died: 23 April 1984
Best known as: Artist, historian and poet
Also: As a painter he was a surrealist but during the Second World War he was a teacher of camouflage
Link with area: He taught military camouflage at the Home Guard training centre at Osterley Park

Piccadilly Line

Hounslow East: Phil Collins

Birth Name: Philip David Charles Collins
Born: 30 January 1951
Best known as: Drummer, singer-songwriter and actor
Also: He was the drummer of rock band Genesis and has been a solo performer since 1981. He's won seven Grammy Awards six Brit Awards amongst others. His hits include In the Air Tonight and Another Day in Paradise
Link with area: He lived there

Hounslow Central: Elvis Costello

Birth Name: Declan Patrick MacManus
Born: 25 August 1954
Best known as: Singer-songwriter
Also: With his backing band The Attractions, his third album Armed Forces features his highest charting single Oliver's Army. In 2008 he was awarded an honorary degree of Doctor of Music by the University of Liverpool (his hometown)
Link with area: He attended St Mark's Catholic School there

Piccadilly Line

Hounslow West: Charles Hawtrey

Birth Name: George Frederick Joffre Hartree
Born: 30 November 1914. Died: 27 October 1988
Best known as: Comedy actor
Also: Best known in the Carry On films, he appeared in more than 70 films including Alfred Hitchcock's Sabotage. In the late Sixties, he moved to Deal in Kent, reputedly because of the sailors in the local naval base
Link with area: He was born there

Piccadilly Line

Hatton Cross: Sir Frederick Pollock

Birth Name: Jonathan Frederick Pollock
Born: 23 September 1783. Died: 28 August 1870
Best known as: 1st Baronet, lawyer and politician
Also: He served, various periods, between 1834 and 1844, as Attorney General in
the tory administration of Sir Robert Peel
Link with area: He lived there

Piccadilly Line

Heathrow Terminals 2&3: Brian Trubshaw

Birth Name: Ernest Brian Trubshaw
Born: 29 January 1924. Died: 24 March 2001
Best known as: test pilot who was the first pilot to fly Concorde in April 1969
Also: He flew in Bomber Command during the Second World War
Link with area: He flew Concorde from Heathrow

Piccadilly Line

Heathrow Terminal 4: Gina Lollobrigida

Birth Name: Luigia Lollobrigida
Born: 4 July 1927
Best known as: Actress
Also: She appeared films such as The World's Most Beautiful Woman (1955),
Trapeze (1956) and Buona Sera, Mrs Campbell (1968) and was nominated three
times for the Golden Globe and won in 1961 as World Film Favorite. Later, she was
known as a photojournalist. In the 1970s she gained access to Fidel Castro for an
exclusive interview
Link with area: She would have often used Heathrow during the course of her
transatlantic travels

Piccadilly Line

Heathrow Terminal 5: Javier Bardem

Birth Name: Javier Ángel Encinas Bardem
Born: 1 March 1969
Best known as: Actor
Also: He won the Academy Award, BAFTA and Golden Globe for Best Supporting
Actor as the psychopathic assassin in No Country for Old Men
Link with area: He frequently uses the airport on his travels

Piccadilly Line

Ealing Common: Ivor Biggun

Birth Name: Robert Doc Cox, also known as Doc Cox
Born: 1 July 1946
Best known as: Musician, singer-songwriter of humorous, smutty songs
Also: He appeared on TV's That's Life for ten years and is active in several pub bands including the Trembling Wheelbarrows. The Winker's Song (Misprint) reached number 22 in the UK Singles Chart. He often collaborated with Judge Dread and Screaming Lord Sutch
Link with area: He lived there while working at the BBC

Piccadilly Line

North Ealing: Peter Crouch

Birth Name: Peter James Crouch
Born: 30 January 1981
Best known as: Professional footballer capped 42 times for England
Also: he has played for Tottenham Hotspur, Queens park Rangers, Portsmouth, Aston Villa, Southampton, Liverpool, Stoke city and Burnley. He regularly appears on BBC Television
Link with area: He attended primary school there

Park Royal: Lord Davies of Abersoch

Birth Name: Evan Mervyn Davies
Born: 21 November 1952
Best known as: Banker and politician formerly Minister of State for Trade, Investment and Small Business
Also: He serves on the Board of Directors for Diageo, a multinational beverage alcohol company
Link with area: Diageo's head office is there

Piccadilly Line

Alperton: Gary Waddock

Birth Name: Gary Patrick Waddock
Born: 17 March 1962
Best known as: Former professional footballer
Also: Mainly played for Queens Park Rangers (1979 - 1987) and Luton Town (1994-1998) and is currently the assistant head coach for Cambridge United
Link with area: He grew up in Alperton

Piccadilly Line

Sudbury Town: Jack Slipper

Birth Name: Jack Kenneth Slipper
Born: 20 April 1924. Died: 24 August 2005
Best known as: Detective Chief Superintendent in the Metropolitan Police in
London who tracked down Ronnie Biggs after the Great Train robbery in 1963
Also: He was involved in the investigation of the The Shepherd's Bush Murders in
which three unarmed policemen were shot dead in 1966
Link with area: He was a member of Sudbury Golf Club

Piccadilly Line

Sudbury Hill: Nicky Hopkins

Birth Name: Nicholas Christian Hopkins
Born: 24 February 1944. Died: 6 September 1994
Best known as: Pianist and organist, playing in sessions with many bands including The Rolling Stones, The Who and The Kinks
Also: He credited his success at curing his addictions to alcohol and drugs to being a Scientologist
Link with area: He attended Sudbury Primary School

South Harrow: Screaming Lord Sutch

Birth Name: David Edward Sutch
Born: 10 November 1940. Died: 16 June 1999
Best known as: Musician and founder of the Official Monster Raving Loony Party
Also: He worked with many musicians including Jeff Beck, Jimmy Page and Ritchie Blackmore and is known for his 1963 novelty hit Jack The Ripper
Link with area: He lived and died there

Piccadilly Line

Rayners Lane: Dev Patel

Birth Name: Dev Patel
Born: 23 April 1990
Best known as: Actor
Also: Famous for his role in Slumdog Millionaire, he has won many awards including a BAFTA for Lion, and Critics Choice and Black Reel Awards for Slumdog Millionaire
Link with area: He lived there

Piccadilly Line

Eastcote: Michael Tippett

Birth Name: Michael Kemp Tippett
Born: 2 January 1905. Died: 8 January 1998
Best known as: Composer
Also: Best known for A Child of Our Time, Fantasia Concertante on a Theme of Corelli and The Midsummer Marriage. He is ranked alongside Benjamin Britten as one of the leading composers of the twentieth century
Link with area: He was born there

Piccadilly Line

Ruislip Manor: Mary, Lady Bankes

Birth Name: Mary Hawtrey, Mary, Lady Bankes
Born: c. 1598. Died: 11 April 1661
Best known as: Royalist who defended Corfe Castle during English Civil War
Also: She was married to Sir John Banks , Lord Chief Justice of the Common Pleas
and Attorney-General of King Charles I. She and her maidservants drove
Parliamentarians away from Corfe Castle with cannon fire
Link with area: She died and was buried there

Piccadilly Line

Ruislip: Peter Levi

Birth Name: Peter Chad Tigar Levi
Born: 16 may 1931. Died: 1 February 2000
Best known as: Poet, archaeologist and Jesuit priest. Two of his poetry collections are called Death is a Pulpit and Life is a Platform
Also: He trained for the priesthood but resigned 29 years later. He was quite an unruly novice during his training possibly an expression of doubts about his vocation. He was professor of poetry at Oxford University from 1984 - 1989.
Link with area: He was born there

Piccadilly Line

Hillingdon: James Corden

Birth Name: James Kimberley Corden
Born: 22 August 1978
Best known as: Actor, comedian and television host
Also: Currently best known as host of the Late Late Show with James Corden in America, he also wrote and starred in Gavin and Stacey after appearing on stage and on film in Alan Bennett's The History Boys. He is the recipient of many awards including BAFTAs and Emmys
Link with area: he was born there

Piccadilly Line

Uxbridge: Christine Keeler

Birth Name: Christine Margaret Keeler
Born: 22 February 1942. Died: 4 December 2017
Best known as: Model and ShowgirlAlso: She became sexually involved with both a Cabinet minister, John Profumo and a Soviet naval attaché, Yevgeny Ivanov at the height of the Cold War, leading to a press investigation into threats to national security
Link with area: She was born there

Victoria Line

Walthamstow: William Morris

Birth Name: William Morris
Born: 24 March 1834. Died: 3 October 1896
Best known as: Textile designer, poet and artist
Also: A socialist activist associated with the Arts and Crafts Movement, he wrote novels and poetry including *The Wood Beyond The World* and *The Well at the World's End*. He created over 600 designs for wallpaper, textiles and embroideries, 150 stained glass windows, three typefaces and 650 borders for the Kelmscott Press
Link with area: He was born there and lived during his teenage years in Water House which has now become the William Morris Gallery

Blackhorse Road: Hayden Thorpe

Birth Name: Hayden Norman Thorpe
Born: 18 January 1986
Best known as: Singer-songwriter with recent albums being Diviner and Moondust for my Diamond
Also: Was the frontman for indie pop band Wild Beasts and then went solo with the aforementioned album Diviner
Link with area: He occasionally works at Blackhorse Road Workshop

Victoria Line

Tottenham Hale: Bernie Grant

Birth Name: Bernard Alexander Montgomery Grant
Born: 17 February 1944. Died: 8 April 2000
Best known as: Politician (Labour Party)
Also: During the 1985 Broadwater Farm riot in which policeman Keith Blakelock
was murdered, he was widely quoted as saying: " What the police got was a
bloody good hiding" when he meant that that was the opinion of the rioters
Link with area: He was council leader for Tottenham

Victoria Line

Seven Sisters: Shirley Bassey

Birth Name: Shirley Veronica Bassey
Born: 8 January 1937
Best known as: Singer
Also: She sang the theme songs to the James Bond films Goldfinger, Diamonds
Are Forever and Moonraker and has had numerous BBC television specials.
Link with area: She has lived there

Victoria Line

Finsbury Park: Jeremy Corbyn

Birth Name: Jeremy Bernard Corbyn
Born: 26 May 1949
Best known as: British politician who was the leader of the Labour party from 2015 - 2020
Also: The initial enthusiasm for his leadership inspired Corbynmania with a repeated chant of "Oh, Jeremy Corbyn" common at many gatherings including Glastonbury.
Link with area: He lives there

Victoria Line

Highbury and Islington: Nick Hornby

Birth Name: Nicholas Peter John Hornby
Born: 17 April 1957
Best known as: Writer and lyricist
Also: Best known for his novels Fever Pitch, High Fidelity and About a Boy, all made into feature films. His awards include The E. M. Forster Award (1999) and the WH Smith Literary Award (2002, for How To be Good)
Link with area: He lives in the area and is a fan of the local team, Arsenal

Victoria Line

Green Park: Peter Langan

Birth Name: Peter Langan
Born: 1941. Died: 7 December 1988 in a fire at his home which he is thought to have started himself
Best known as: Entrepreneur who opened Langan's Brasserie in Mayfair in partnership with Michael Caine
Also: Renowned for his hell-raising antics such as crawling under the tables biting unsuspecting female diners' ankles
Link with area: Langan's Brasserie is just around the corner from the station

278

Victoria: Ian Fleming

Birth Name: Ian Lancaster Fleming
Born: 28 May 1908. Died: 12 August 1964
Best known as: Writer and journalist, creator of the James Bond series of novels
Also: He was involved in the planning of Operation Goldeneye whilst serving in the
Naval Intelligence Division during the Second World War
Link with area: He lived at 22 Ebury Street in the area

Victoria Line

Pimlico: Paul Weller

Birth Name: Paul John Weller
Born: 25 May 1958
Best known as: Singer-songwriter and musician
Also: Achieved fame with The Jam and the Style Council before going solo with the hits You Do Something To Me and Town Called Malice, becoming known as the 'Modfather' and being an influence on Britpop bands such as Oasis. He has received four Brit Awards
Link with area: As he said: "When I lived in a little flat in Pimlico in 1981, I'd write in the hallway. As you walked in, there was a tiny little recess type thing, hardly a hallway, really, and I'd sit there writing songs with my guitar"

Victoria Line

Vauxhall: Florence Eshalomi

Birth Name: Florence Dauta Eshalomi (née Nosegbe)
Born: 18 September 1980
Best known as: Politican serving as an MP for Vauxhall since 2019
Also: Currently on the Labour Party frontbencher as Deputy Leader, Angela Rayner's Parliamentary Private Secretary
Link with area: At the time of writing she is the MP for the area

Victoria Line

Brixton: David Bowie

Birth Name: David Robert Jones
Born: 8 January 1947. Died: 10 January 2016
Best known as: Singer-songwriter and actor regarded as one of the most influential musicians of the 20th century
Also: Starting with Space Oddity in 1969, he went thought various guises such as Ziggy Stardust with songs such as Starman, The Jean Genie, Life on Mars and Rebel Rebel. The multi-talented artist was also a multiple award winner and as an actor he appeared in The Man Who Fell To Earth, Christiane F. and Absolute Beginners amongst others.
Link with area: He was born in Stansfield Road, Brixton

Who's FAMOUS at your STATION?

Index: Stations

283

Index: Stations

Who's FAMOUS at your STATION?

Who's FAMOUS at your STATION?

Index: Stations

Index: Stations

Who's FAMOUS at your STATION?

Who's FAMOUS at your STATION?

Index: Stations

Index: Stations

Who's FAMOUS at your STATION?

Printed in Great Britain
by Amazon

84439946R00165